92
Hol   Judson, Clara

        Mr. Justice Holmes

    cl

92
Hol

    Judson, Clara
    Mr. Justice Holmes.

Mr. Justice Holmes

by Clara Ingram Judson

Mr. Justice Holmes

Illustrated by Robert Todd

Follett Publishing Company   CHICAGO

Author's Foreword

In prehistoric times, when men began to live together in groups, they felt the need for simple rules to govern their behavior. These rules became tribal laws, and as the groups grew into larger communities, more laws were needed. To primitive peoples, tribal laws were extremely important; they were strictly kept, and those who broke the law were severely punished — often with death for what might seem to us a trifling offense.

As society became more complicated, more laws were necessary. Thoughtful men knew that law was the force which held civilization together, and they strove to make wise and just laws.

With the coming of the industrial era, laws multiplied. Perhaps because of the very numbers, a measure of respect for law was lost; its meaning as the foundation of social order was obscured. Some citizens acted as though breaking a law — perhaps by a traffic violation — was a challenge. This dangerous perverseness became the theme of countless articles in magazines and newspapers as people began to see that lawlessness of a few was endangering the many.

Reading and thinking on these matters brought a desire to contribute in some way to a wider understanding and respect for law. My way of contributing has always been through my writing. What kind of book could I write that would make readers appreciate the lofty place of law in the lives of all of us? It seemed to me that the complex subject of law might become simple and human if viewed through the life and work of some great man in the legal profession.

The United States has produced many brilliant lawyers who became judges, among them John Marshall, Roger Taney, Oliver Wendell Holmes, Jr., and Charles Evans Hughes. After much study I chose Holmes: lawyer and jurist, judge and justice, philosopher and writer, and above all, a courageous man who believed that law was for all the people.

As I read and studied, I was more than happy that I had chosen to write about Wendell Holmes. No other American could better have suited my purpose, for Holmes himself spent the greater part of his long life in studying law, in working to make such laws as would command the respect of men, and in securing through law the greatest good for the greatest number. His outstanding contribution was in showing that law is not a dull, static thing, but experimental, fluid, realistic. His courage and faith and human understanding and the splendid language of his opinions still remain an inspiration on the bench of the highest court of the United States, where he served with honor for thirty years.

As always in the writing of authentic biography, I am indebted to many kind people who have helped me in the search for truth. Among these are Mr. C. P. Cullinan, Assistant Clerk of the United States Supreme Court, who was generous with his time and his knowledge of federal courts; Mr. E. Kelly, Assistant Clerk of the Superior Court of the County of Suffolk of the Commonwealth of Massachusetts, who let me see the original docket of Wendell Holmes taking the lawyer's oath, March 4, 1867, and other papers; and Mr. Kimball C. Elkins, Senior Assistant in the Harvard University Archives, who showed me valuable papers and clippings and gave me permission to quote from the volume of Class of 1861 biographies. My thanks also to the Harvard University Press for permission to quote from Holmes' Memorial Day speech (1884) and from the war diary and the letters published under the title *Touched With Fire*.

Among many libraries visited were the Massachusetts Historical Society, the Boston Athenaeum, the Bostonian Club, and the Boston Public Library, where Miss Swift in the Rare Book Room and Miss Lang in the Reference Room were especially helpful. And as always, I am grateful to Deering Library, Northwestern University, and Miss Perkins, and to the Evanston Public Library, Miss Borchelt and Miss Davison, for unfailing inspiration and help.

C.I.J.

Evanston, Illinois

May 23, 1956

Mr. Justice Holmes

The State House

A Boston Boy

1

The long expected day had come — October 25, 1848 — one of the important days in Boston's history. Schools were closed; many pupils were to march in the parade that celebrated the turning on of Boston's new city water system.

As people left their homes they rejoiced that it was such a beautiful day. Sunshine glittered on the golden dome of the State House. A brisk breeze from the bay held hundreds of flags out against a bright blue sky. By horse and buggy and on foot people hurried toward the Common and adjoining streets to get good positions for watching the parade.

Below the steps of number 8 Montgomery Street, near the Park Street Church, small Amelia Holmes waited impatiently. Suddenly she heard a band.

"Mother!" she shouted. "It's coming. Wendell must hurry!"

"I'm here!" Wendell Holmes called from the front stairway. He smiled at his mother as he dashed by, clattered down the stone steps and grabbed Amelia's hand.

"We've plenty of time," he said reassuringly. "That band must be going to join up with its division."

Amelia looked up at her brother with trust. He was a tall lad for his less than eight years. Dark hair dropped over a high forehead and his gray-blue eyes sparkled with excitement.

The two turned and waved to their mother, who was staying at home with baby Edward. Then they ran to Tremont Street, turned the corner, and made for a place across from the Common.

Sidewalks were crowded, but Wendell wangled a spot for Amelia and pulled her to the place he chose above the gutter. He put his hand on her shoulder to keep her close; then he looked around. Yes, they were in ample time. Crowds were still milling about, everyone in a gay mood.

Soon church bells rang. A cannon boomed, and a band playing stirring martial music drew near. The crowd stilled, waiting.

This was no ordinary parade, usual enough this campaign year, when partisans for the Mexican War hero, Old Zach Taylor, or Michigan's favorite son, Lewis Cass, turned out. No, this was a parade to celebrate the success of a huge civic project — the bringing of fresh, pure water to Boston. This was a day when everyone, no matter of what political membership, could rejoice.

For years men had been planning and gangs of other men had been digging to bring water from the Cochituate, fifteen miles westward, to growing Boston. Now that huge task was done.

"The parade's coming!" Those tall enough to see banners
passed the word along. People crowded to the front as the
first of eight divisions came abreast.

It was a wonderful parade! Handsome floats represented
the history of the waterworks project. Various societies had
floats, too. Distinguished guests rode in carriages, the horses
prancing nervously because red, white, and blue paper pompons
rustled on their harnesses. The faculty of Harvard University
marched in a body, very elegant and impressive in long morning coats and high silk hats.

"There's Father!" Amelia cried and rose on tiptoe to wave
at a small man in the center of a line.

Perhaps he heard her, for he smiled and waved. Unlike
other professors, Wendell noticed, his father did not march
in dignified silence, eyes front. He watched the crowd, he
bowed and waved here and there, enjoying himself.

"Who is that?" Wendell heard a voice behind him ask.

"That's the famous Dr. Oliver Wendell Holmes — you've
heard of him — poet, lecturer, doctor. Look while you have
the chance to see him!"

Oliver Wendell Holmes, Junior, flushed. People were
always talking about his father! Yet his father was neither em-
barrassed nor annoyed. He looked pleased. Even now, when
others were solemn, Dr. Holmes was chatting with his march-
ing-mate and enjoying himself.

"Come on, Wendie!" A friend pulled at Wendell's elbow.
"They'll be turning the water on!"

"I have to take Amelia home first," Wendell remembered.

The parade had passed. The crowd was thinning out,
and people rushed across the Common for the exercises.

"I don't want to go home," Amelia said firmly.

"Mother will give you a cookie," Wendell promised, and
suddenly Amelia felt hungry and went with him.

Wendell raced back to his friend, and they hurried across to find a place in the section reserved for children who were not in the parade.

They were in plenty of time. The parade had wound through old Boston, passed Faneuil Hall and back. Ten can-

non shots announced the arrival on the Common, thrilling, terrifying sounds, but it was some time after that before the
audience was in its place. No horses were allowed on the
Common, so the Chief Marshal and his aides had to dismount,
reform, and march with music to a stand by the Pond where
the exercises were to be. Wendell Holmes and his friends
watched all this with lively interest.

With the singing of a hymn, the crowd quieted. There
was a prayer and the reading of an ode which the poet James
Russell Lowell had written for this day. The report of the
hard-working waterworks committee was read, and the Mayor
spoke.

Then, with a proud gesture, he turned a valve, and water
piped from so far away, shot upward, higher and higher.

"I'll bet that's eighty feet high!" a guard cried, awed.

"Look at her go!" boys yelled.

The breeze blew mist and spray over the watchers. No
one cared; wetness was an added thrill. Only in Boston could
such a wonder as this happen.

A roll of drums quieted the talk, and a great choir ended
the exercises with singing of a chorus from Elijah, "Thanks be
to God for he laveth the thirsty land."

The hush was broken with satisfied talk.

"Boston does things right!"

"Not another city in the land can get ahead of us!"

Gradually most of the crowd scattered. The school boys
stayed and watched the waterworks men turn off the water and
finish up the job.

The next morning, Wendell Holmes went to school again. Like other boys he knew, he attended a dame school. Several of these private primary schools were held in the back parlors of fine old houses near the Common. In dame schools, New England gentlewomen taught young pupils reading, writing, and ciphering. Wendell did not need to be taught reading; he had read ever since he could remember. But writing and ciphering were work.

This morning, after the thrill of the parade, it was hard to settle down and listen to his teacher.

"Rest your hand on your third and fourth fingers, Wendell," she said. "So . . . touch the desk only with those fingers and your under arm — see? Now, rotate. Easy now, rotate." She guided his hand in a circling motion, round and round and round. Wendell was sure he made miles and miles of circles, rotating. His teacher kept him at it day after day until he learned to write a clear, flowing script, like engraving, easy to read and to write. Ciphering was almost as hard, too.

So it was a pleasure to come home on a day not long after the celebration, and find his father's horse and buggy in front of his home and his father coming out of the front door.

"Want to drive to Cambridge with me and see your Grandmother Holmes?" Dr. Holmes asked.

"Oh, yes, Father," Wendell's eyes brightened. "And maybe Uncle John will be there, too."

"Maybe. Maybe not. Climb in, Son." And off they sped. Dr. Holmes was a good judge of horses and always had a fast one to get him to the hospital where he studied and taught, to the Harvard Medical College where he had classes in anatomy, to Harvard College in Cambridge where he was an officer, and to his many friends and various engagements. Dr. Holmes liked to be "on the go" as people called it.

Now the buggy whisked around corners, over the West Boston Bridge and out to Harvard Square. The Holmes' house, where Dr. Holmes had been born, was nearby. Wendell jumped out and his father drove on to his engagement.

Wendell climbed the steps and shook the brass knocker in pleased anticipation of his grandmother's surprise. Uncle John was not at home, but Grandmother was delighted to see him.

Sarah Wendell Holmes, widow of Abiel, the preacher and historian, was a tiny woman with bright dark eyes and endless energy. She always had apples and cookies and comfortable talk, and she never asked questions as Wendell's father did: "What boys did you play with today?" "What did you learn that was new?" She let Wendell choose his own talk. This day he was eager to tell her about the waterworks celebration, the parade, and the high stream of water that misted over the people.

"You know, Wendell," she remarked when he paused to eat, "Boston has changed more since you were born, let's see, March 8th in '41, than in all the years since the Revolutionary War. That was a long time ago — but I remember it well. I was little Sally Wendell when the redcoats came marching in to Boston. My father, Judge Oliver Wendell, the man you and your father are named for, happened to be at home when people came rushing madly along the street shouting that the British had come; that they were murdering everyone they saw. I didn't exactly know what murdering was, but I knew that it was bad. Funny, now that I tell it, that doesn't seem as long ago as it really was." Then she noticed the vanishing cookies.

"You were hungry, Wendell. Would you like some pie?" He nodded, mouth full. She brought from the pantry a plate with a big wedge of pumpkin pie, set it before him and laid

beside it a hand-hammered silver fork marked with a W.

Wendell's eyes brightened, and he began to eat the pie. His grandmother talked on, bringing the war directly into this very house.

"General Ward lived in this house then," she said. "There were very few buildings near, so from the west windows he could see toward Concord and Lexington. From the east he might have seen sails on the river while he was planning the defense near Bunker Hill. George Washington lived nearby after he took over command of the army. Soldiers were in and out of this house. Look, Wendell. You can see the marks of muskets on the floor. I never could sand them away though I've tried."

Wendell got up and looked. He bent over and touched the little hollows she pointed out.

"I don't try to rub those marks away any more. I'm proud of them in a way," she added. "It doesn't seem long ago — not when you live in this house."

"Did General Ward mind a little girl living here?" Wendell asked.

"Oh, we lived in Boston then — didn't anyone ever tell you? That's why we were so close to the British redcoats. The rebel army was here, in Cambridge. After I grew up your grandfather and I were married the month that Thomas Jefferson became president, and we moved to this house at the time he put his embargo on shipping. Mr. Jefferson always seemed connected with us somehow. Most of the people we knew thought he was a dangerous man — always talking about the common people and their rights. It was the fashion in Boston then to think that only educated people had rights, especially the right to rule. How Tom Jefferson could be a Virginian and as queer as he was, no one understood. But he didn't ruin the country after all. We came out pretty well. You live in a good country.

"Want something more, Wendell?" The boy shook his head — he was no longer hungry.

"Your grandfather was fair about Jefferson when he wrote his history of the country. Fair about the British, too. Some day you must look at that history book, Wendell. He worked hard writing it, and reviewers called it honest history."

"May I see it now?" Wendell asked, intrigued.

"Why, yes, if you want to. It's upstairs in the library where he wrote it."

Wendell followed her upstairs and into the library at the front of the house. She went to the old desk, picked up a book and opened it at the title page. Wendell read:

ANNALS OF HISTORY

BY

Abiel Holmes, D.D.

"That's my grandfather!" he said. "I didn't know he wrote a history book."

"Time you knew," Mrs. Holmes smiled at him. "How hard he worked to have that book true and fair! He had boxes full of books and notes — long before he began to write."

"Why did he care so much?" Wendell wanted to know.

"Partly because he loved his country. Partly because of his father. David Holmes was a soldier. He fought long and bravely in the French and Indian War and in the Revolution. After the wars were won, David had a hard time living with his old wounds and illnesses and troubles the wars had made him suffer. But David Holmes didn't fuss. He'd got what he wanted most — a good country to live in. Men cared a lot about their country then. Nowadays there seems nothing so im-

portant to care about — building mills, piping water — those
are good things, but your country is *important!*"

Wendell liked the sound of her words, but he only half
listened, for he was turning the pages of the Annals.

"May I read the book now, Grandmother?" he asked.

"Yes, if you like. Your father won't come for a while yet.
You see there is something for each year, beginning with Colum-
bus. Maybe you'd like to turn to 1775 and read about the war
that was fought around here."

"I'd rather begin at the beginning. I'd like to know about
it all, Grandmother." He was absorbed in reading of the year
1497 when she slipped out to get her knitting.

Wendell was still reading and Mrs. Holmes knitting by the
window when she saw her son, Dr. Holmes, drive up.

"You'd better go down quickly," she suggested. "Your
father might be in a hurry."

"May I read the book next time I come, Grandmother?"

"Yes. Put this marker in, and I'll leave it on the desk. You
may read it any time, Wendell."

Dr. Holmes was at the door when Wendell opened it.

"I'm in a hurry, Son. Sorry not to stop, Mother. See
you soon, though."

"Bring Wendell again," Mrs. Holmes called after them.

"What were you doing all this time, Son?" Dr. Holmes
asked as he drove toward Boston.

"I ate. And then I read the *Annals of History.*"

"My father's book?" Dr. Holmes was astonished.

"Yes," Wendell said. "I like it. I'll read more next time."

Dr. Holmes sat, silent. He flicked the whip thoughtfully. Wendell wondered at the silence.

"You've no business in dame school if you can read that history book," he said after a time. "I must see about sending you to Mr. Sullivan. He's a good teacher."

"Yes, sir," Wendell agreed. He was very happy.

2

Latin School

Grandmother Holmes' House

Wendell Holmes was pleased to go to Mr. Sullivan's school. His parents approved it, too, for Mr. Sullivan, unlike many teachers of his day, did not practice flogging students for their faults. He had the new idea that boys might be interested in their studies and behave well by their own choice.

The boys studied Latin and a beginning course in Greek. Mr. Sullivan called ciphering "Mathematics" but the new name did not make the subject any easier for Wendell.

Afternoons and Saturdays, when their chores at home were done, Wendell and his friends played on the Common. This wide, open space in the middle of Boston had originally been set aside for pasturing cows — a fortunate thing, for now it was a city park. Great elms and linden trees made shade in summer, and the slope down from the State House was a fine hill for coasting in winter. Boys not yet skillful enough to dodge trees coasted on the smaller hill by the pond.

In the years that Wendell was in school, boys played

marbles and spun tops; they played "catch," tossing balls to each other. They ran races on the mile-long brick walk around the Common, and gradually these races grew competitive, the winner bringing honor to himself and his school.

When snow covered the Common, coasting — the most exciting sport of the year — challenged every boy. All through the autumn, sleds were made ready. Some were brightly painted. Many had leather trim put on with shining brass or nickel nails. Often boys named their sleds — Ariel, Olympus, or some other classical name.

Wendell Holmes was proud of his sled and his coasting skill. He knew just the instant to drop lightly on the moving sled; the exact shift of his weight that would dodge obstacles and get that extra foot or two of distance that made him win.

These sports were not always played out in peace. The 1840's were hungry years in Ireland because of a dreadful potato blight. Hundreds of Irish families managed to sail to the New World. Many landed at the port of Boston and settled nearby, where the men got work. In the main it was Irishmen who dug canals, laid railroads and water pipes. Their strength helped make possible the rapid growth of Boston and other cities.

Irish lads in the strange new country did not yet have marbles and sleds. In envious groups they gathered around the Common watching sports they did not share. They grew bold and threw sticks and stones at more fortunate boys. In winter they packed snow around stones and made dangerous balls.

Boston boys ignored the strangers when they could; other times they fought back.

"Here come those muckers!" some sharp-eyed lad would shout.

"Give 'em as good as they send," others yelled.

Play hours on the Common were never dull. Many a boy limped home, nursing a hurt leg or a black eye.

This was one reason why school boys' range of interest widened in the spring that Wendell was ten. The other reason was the discovery of gold in California two years earlier.

In those two years a shipbuilding boom had grown on Boston Bay. Boys took to climbing Beacon Hill and watching ships building on the ways and other ships coming and going in the harbor. It was vastly more exciting than playing ball on the Common.

In April of that year, 1851, the *Flying Cloud* was launched from Donald McKay's shipyard in East Boston, and the greatest crowd ever assembled watched her slide down the ways. The harbor was crowded with small boats loaded to the waterline. Many onlookers had driven to the shipyard, and others watched from Beacon Hill where they could see the whole fascinating scene.

"She's the most beautiful ship ever launched!" people said.

"Look at her lines! See how she takes to the water!"

"She'll make a record to San Francisco, I'm guessing!"

And indeed she did. The *Flying Cloud* made the long trip around the Horn in eighty-nine days — a world record that held for many years.

After this day, Wendell Holmes and his friends began to collect flags and insignia of ships. Each merchant had a "line" of ships and each "liner" its own insignia. Enoch Train's line carried a black T on her top foresail; his Liverpool line added a red flag with a white diamond. The Ball line had a great black ball painted on a sail. For advertising, merchants printed slips of paper with their insignia, and boys collected these.

After school Mr. Sullivan's boys climbed the hill overlooking the harbor and vied with each other naming ships they saw, and the lines. Sometimes they boldly walked the wharves where one could smell tea and spices and roasting coffee and see strange, foreign sailors wearing great gold earrings. They collected lychee nuts from China and paper trifles from Japan. The languages the sailors spoke were odd sounding, different from Latin or Greek the boys studied.

Wendell often came home with tales that entertained Amelia or with an extra flag he could spare from his collection.

The Railroad Jubilee, celebrating the joining of an eastern with a western road, was a three-day festival in a tent on the Common. And after that there was a traveling circus. A

thoughtful boy like Wendell became interested in faraway places, especially the distant West.

One day Dr. Holmes came home early and stumbled over Wendell, stretched out on the library floor reading Dana's *Two Years Before the Mast*.

"Really, Son," he said, vexed, "you do nothing but read!"

"I like to read," Wendell said, scrambling to his feet. "But I'm sorry I was on the floor, Father."

"Haven't you studies?"

"No, sir. I've finished today's lessons."

"Then Sullivan is too easy on you. Perhaps you are ready for Latin School. I'll talk to Dixwell about you."

"Yes, sir. I'd like that," Wendell said, pleased.

Epes Dixwell was the headmaster in the excellent Boston Latin School, a high school, and Dr. Holmes had confidence in him. But by the time Dr. Holmes talked with him, Boston politicians had decided that teachers in the Latin School must live in the city of Boston. Mr. Dixwell owned his home in Cambridge, and he had no intention of living in Boston. So he resigned.

Several loyal parents persuaded Mr. Dixwell to open a private school of his own and make his own rules. The schoolmaster liked this idea. He built a fine new school on Boylston Place, beyond the Common. Here he planned to teach upper grades and high school. Wendell Holmes was one of the more than fifty boys enrolled in that school its first day. They milled around the school yard, eyeing each other, as they waited for the master to arrive.

"Here he comes!" The word was whispered around.

Play stopped as boys watched the headmaster walk near. Wendell stared, astonished; Dr. Holmes wore severe black suits, every day. Epes Dixwell's light-colored overcoat hung open, showing a bright green waistcoat, a purple suit coat and vivid, checked trousers.

"My brother says the master is color blind," a boy whispered to Wendell. "We can have fun with him — about colors, you know."

Just then the bell rang and boys flocked in to find their seats. The master's eye wandered around the room gently; whispering stopped. Wendell thought this was not a man to have fun with about either clothes or colors.

Silently the boys watched the schoolmaster remove his glasses and lay them on his desk; pick up a Bible and begin to read from the first chapter of Genesis. After the first sentence he stopped and looked up.

"That sentence is the most sublime sentence in the English language. Remember it." And he read on. Not a boy moved.

Dixwell prayed briefly, and the year's work began.

Wendell found he was to continue Latin and Greek as a gentleman should. He had more mathematics and began French; later he would study some ancient history. Of course students were taught no modern history, and as for American history, it was not mentioned. Wendell would not have known anything about his country but for his reading in his grandmother's library.

Now that he was in Latin School, Wendell was allowed

to walk to Cambridge by himself to visit Grandmother Holmes. The three-mile journey took more than an hour because he liked to linger on the bridge and watch shipping in the bay. Mrs. Holmes fed him and let him browse in the big library. Sometimes she came in and chatted with him. It was from Grandmother and Uncle John, Dr. Holmes' younger unmarried brother, a lawyer, that Wendell came to know his father.

"Your grandfather, Abiel Holmes, was a Connecticut man so of course he went to Yale," Mrs. Holmes told Wendell. "But your father went to Harvard — we lived here, then."

"My father is a famous man, isn't he, Grandmother?" Wendell remarked, after a pause.

"Yes, I think you could say that he's famous. It happened suddenly, when he was only twenty-one years old. We'd known he had an easy way with words, but he was studying law and we didn't think about writing.

"Then, unexpectedly word got around that the old *Constitution,* the warship that Americans loved, was going to be scrapped. People around here were furious — but what could they do? The order had passed. Your father wrote a poem — you know it, Wendell, though perhaps we never told you the story." She recited the first verse:

> *Aye! Tear her tattered ensign down*
> *Long has it waved on high,*
> *And many an eye has danced to see*
> *That banner in the sky!*

"He wrote it quickly, in pencil, as though it just spilled out of his mind and heart.

"Some friend dashed off with it, and before we knew it the poem was printed in the newspaper and everyone was talking about it. Next thing Boston people knew, handbills with the poem were printed in Washington, and so many people were stirred that the order to scrap the ship was cancelled — and your father suddenly had a kind of fame." Wendell made no comment.

"But Father isn't a lawyer," he remarked later.

"No, he didn't like the law, so he studied medicine."

"He doesn't go to see sick people, Grandmother."

"No, he didn't like practicing medicine, Wendell. He moved to Boston so he could be near the hospital. He liked studying illnesses and teaching young men who were to be doctors. And he did more writing, too. Your father has many skills, Wendell.

"When he married your mother, her father, Judge Jackson, gave them the house where you live for a wedding present. It suits your father to live in Boston. Your father is a friendly, sociable man, a good talker, too. People like him," she added proudly.

On the long walk home, that day, Wendell tried to think of his father as his Grandmother saw him; but he couldn't. Still less could he understand when he went down to breakfast the next morning.

During Wendell's boyhood, breakfast was the important family meal in the Holmes household. Guests were frequent at dinners and suppers, and then of course children were silent. They sat at table, they heard good talk — no table in Boston

had better. But talk was between grownups; children did not
share it.

Breakfast was different. Then Dr. Holmes devoted himself
to his children. He came to the table briskly. Wendell marveled
at his father's energy and vigor. The boy was growing fast; he
never wanted to get up, he dressed slowly and painfully,
dragged himself down the stairs to the dining room.

"Late again," Dr. Holmes commented this particular morn-
ing. "There is no sense in being late — ever. You were called.
I expect you to be seated before the porridge is brought in."
He stared at his son in disfavor. The boy was already his

father's height — five foot four — and seemed about to pass
him. That thought did not add to the doctor's pleasure.

Wendell slid into his chair and began eating. Amelia
smiled at him as she sprinkled brown sugar on her porridge.
Young Edward made a nice diversion by spilling his milk.
When the mess was cleaned up, Dr. Holmes helped himself
to marmalade from the glass jar in the center of the table.

"Now perhaps we can have quiet," he began. "Wendell,
tell me what you learned yesterday. Maybe you can get the
double serving of marmalade today — Amelia enjoyed it yesterday."

Wendell swallowed hard. That extra spoonful, his father's
daily prize for the brightest remark made by one of the three
children, always dismayed him. The very thought of it seemed
to stupefy his mind.

Let Amelia get it again, he thought. Who cares?

But his father was waiting. What *had* they studied?

"We studied Latin, as always," Wendell said. "And Mr.
Dixwell showed us a picture of the Forum."

"For 'em Romans!" Dr. Holmes quipped gleefully.

Wendell winced. Such a terrible pun! For an instant he
thought he could not bear to stay at the table.

Amelia laughed. She did not understand a pun, good or
bad, but she could tell by her father's face that a laugh was
expected. Edward grinned.

"That's a good one, Father," he said agreeably.

"And *you* get the marmalade today, Edward. Your sentence is the best I have heard this morning." Dr. Holmes

spooned jam onto Edward's plate. Then he eyed his older son in vexation.

"Wendell, can't you get a collar to cover your neck? One thing is certain, you will never make a successful public speaker. Your neck is too long. No audience could ever stand the sight of it!"

Wendell flushed scarlet. As soon as he dared he excused himself and left the table.

That afternoon he hurried home from school and hunted up his mother in her little sewing room.

"Is my neck really too long, Mother?" he asked anxiously. "Will my ugly looks keep me from having a good life?"

"Certainly not!" she exclaimed quickly. "You know your father speaks hastily sometimes; you are foolish to heed such words. Boys grow by spurts. By the time you are a man your neck will be right for the rest of you. In a few years you will be a handsome man, Son. And remember this, you can be or do what you choose — looks make little difference. It's your mind and will that count."

Wendell straightened his shoulders, and the anxious look left his face.

"Thank you, Mother," he said. "I wondered . . ." He smiled at her and dashed off to join the boys on the Common.

That boy, his mother thought, as through a mist of unshed tears she threaded her needle. His father doesn't understand him, and he doesn't understand his father.

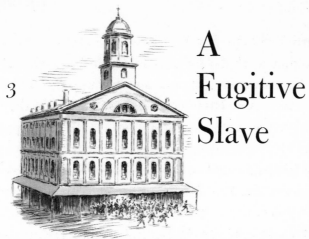

A Fugitive Slave

Faneuil Hall

By the spring of 1854, when Wendell was thirteen, he had grown so tall that he towered over every other member of his family.

"I don't see where you get this tallness!" his mother complained as she inspected the sleeves of his best coat and saw that they could not be let down any more. "He will have to have a new suit for Sundays," she added to her husband.

"It would be a good thing if you did some growing in your mind," Dr. Holmes remarked in an irritated tone. "I got your monthly report yesterday, and I do not like it."

Wendell flushed but could think of nothing to say. The report was average, not disgraceful. But his father expected a son to stand at the top, and Wendell was only middling.

"Edward does much better at Mr. Sullivan's. I know he will make us proud of him when he goes to Dixwell."

"Yes, sir, I'm sure he will," Wendell agreed and went up to his room.

There, looking over the roofs and chimneys he wondered why he didn't work harder at school. He liked Mr. Dixwell; he didn't mind the work. But nothing there interested him as much as reading at home. He liked to browse along the shelves in his father's large and well chosen library. He liked to pick a book that looked interesting and take it upstairs to read. Often he read late into the night, if he liked a book, and then was dull and sleepy at school — no one bothered to ask him why.

Sometimes, for a change, he picked out a shelf and read straight through taking books as they came. He borrowed from his Grandmother Holmes' good library, too. But none of his reading showed up in improved marks given for Greek and Latin and ancient history.

This spring Wendell discovered newspapers. Several were published in Boston; Wendell had paid no attention to them before. Now he carried them to his room and pored over the long columns of fine print. They accumulated in piles until his mother raided his room when she needed fresh covers for shelves.

Along in May Wendell noticed an article about a "fugitive slave." Fugitive — from his Latin he knew the meaning of that word for runaway — it was interesting to find it in the newspaper. Intrigued, he read on.

A slave, Anthony Burns, had run away from Virginia, the story said. He had been discovered in Boston, and his master had come to take him back. Meanwhile the slave was held in the courthouse jail, the cold, dreary basement of the courthouse known as the Tombs because it was more like a mausoleum than a place for living human beings.

One of Wendell's friends had read the newspaper too, and after school they walked by the courthouse. People were busily coming and going. The scene was livelier than usual. The boys overheard bits of talk as men passed by.

"Abolitionists will make a case out of this."

"Ought to buy the man and free him."

"Garrison and Parker will inflame the crowds and make trouble."

"Father knows those men," Wendell remarked as the boys walked on. "They want to free all slaves right off."

"My father says that would take a mint of money," Wendell's friend said. "Come on, there's nothing exciting here; let's go down to the Long Wharf and see what's come in."

At supper that evening Wendell listened avidly to the spirited talk.

"If they make a scene as they did in '51 with Simms, Boston will see trouble."

Simms — oh yes, Wendell remembered. He was a runaway slave, too. His master had come north for him. Simms had been carted, in irons, to a ship which sailed off south. Three years ago Wendell had not been reading newspapers, nor had he any interest in civic affairs. Now he listened closely.

"This time it will turn out all right," Dr. Holmes was saying. "Money is now being raised to buy the man. He will be set free."

"Dr. Holmes!" the voice was loud and angry. "Do you consent to the sale of a slave in *Boston?*"

Men turned in their chairs, forks in air, to stare.

"But it's to free the man!" someone exclaimed.

"It's none the less selling a slave in our fair city."

"What would *you* do?"

"Get him out of jail. *Give* him his freedom. Never buy it!" The speaker swung his arm, knocking over his glass.

"Wendell, I'm sure you have studying to do," Mrs. Holmes whispered. "You may be excused."

Wendell had no choice but to leave the table and drag himself upstairs to his Greek homework.

Two days later the papers announced that a meeting was to be held in Faneuil Hall — that famous building often called the cradle of liberty. Theodore Parker and others were to speak.

"First thing you know there will be a mob rushing out of that meeting!" exclaimed Dr. Holmes. He was too disturbed to remember bright sentences and the spoonful of marmalade. Wendell was astonished at the omission of that childish rite.

Boys at school talked as they gathered in the yard. No one knew any facts, and opinions varied. But there was an air of uneasiness in the schoolyard, on the streets, and on the Common.

That evening Wendell finished his homework. His third-floor room felt hot and close in the unusual May heat. He opened the window wider and reached for the book he meant to finish.

Suddenly he heard a roar — a frustrated, human roar — from the direction of the courthouse. He peered out — the place was only a short distance away. A light flared, as from a torch or maybe from many. Then there was darkness.

Surely the street lights are out! Wendell thought.

A loud thump! Thump! Muffled talk. Silence.

He waited by the open window, sensing drama, knowing that he would not be allowed to go from the house. Was it minutes? A half an hour?

The doorbell rang imperatively. He bolted down the stairs but near the top of the second flight he paused. Dr. Holmes had opened the door, was greeting a man whose face was muddied and who clutched a torn coat sleeve as blood dripped onto the floor.

"Can you fix me up?" the man cried. "It's bleeding too much for me to make it home."

"Come right in," Dr. Holmes said. "Things went wrong?"

"The timing was all wrong!" the man cried in a weary voice. "We battered open the courthouse door but they balked us there. Burns is still in jail. We didn't even get inside! Everything was wrong . . ." The door closed. The rumble of low talk came from the study. Mrs. Holmes looked at the big clock.

"It's time for bed, Wendell. Good night, Son."

Reluctantly Wendell turned and climbed the stairs, his lively curiosity making thought of sleep ridiculous.

The next day's newspapers had various accounts of the affair at the courthouse, according to the political ideas of the editors. A brave crowd rushed from Faneuil Hall to free an enslaved man. A murderous mob smashed the courthouse door with a heavy timber, and in the melee a man was killed. Murdered with a gun. Slashed with a cutlass.

Two statements were agreed on: the effort to free Burns failed, and a man was killed.

At supper Dr. Holmes seemed relieved.

"Richard Dana has volunteered to defend Anthony Burns," he told his family and a couple of guests. "Dick will get him free, I have no fear. There's not a shrewder lawyer in the city."

"Well, I don't know," a guest drawled. "Dana will be talking against the federal Fugitive Slave Law — you can't toss off a federal law, Doctor."

"What Dana wants to get into it for is beyond me," the other guest was plainly annoyed. "He's bright. He was getting a fine start in law. And after this not a business man in the city will go to him. I tell you the thing is dangerous."

They were still arguing after the good supper had been eaten and they had moved to the parlor.

Dana was accepted by the judge for the defense attorney — Wendell read this in the paper. His father recounted the tale of the trial a couple of days later.

"Never was there such a day!" Dr. Holmes was excited; he loved drama. "The district attorney got militia out with their guns. They weren't going to let anyone into the courtroom. Dana had to identify himself! Imagine, the lawyer for the defense! But he got in finally. Trust Dana.

"He had a neat defense argument, too. Based on identity."

"What would that be?" Wendell asked.

"Proving who a person is," Dr. Holmes said. "The man who says he is the owner described his slave as a colored man with a scar on his face and a scarred right hand. The man was right there for all to see. Dana pointed to him; pure African Negro; a large scar on his face and his right hand (he had the man hold it up) wasn't scarred. It was mangled, broken, useless. Dana certainly scored with that.

"And as for running away," Dr. Holmes went on as his hearers waited. "The man didn't run away. He was hired out by his master to tote cargo onto a ship and, weary, he sat down in a corner. When he wakened, the ship was under way to Boston. He couldn't walk back."

"Then he'll be freed?" Mrs. Holmes asked anxiously.

"Well, that's not certain. Dana is worried. He says the

judge didn't take a single note while he was summing up the
case. That might mean the judge had his mind already made
up before Dana began. After all, there's the federal law . . .
I'm late to my lecture . . I hope the verdict comes tomorrow!"
He dashed away.

The next day when Wendell came home from school Uncle
John Holmes was just leaving the house.

"Oh, Uncle John!" Wendell's face was radiant. "I do want
to ask you . . ."

"Climb in my buggy and drive to Cambridge with me
then," Uncle John said briskly. "I've got to meet a man. You
won't mind walking home this nice day. Now ask ahead."

Wendell climbed in, and they set off at a brisk trot.

"I want to know what the Fugitive Slave Law is."

"That law is part of a bill passed by Congress called the
Compromise of 1850," Uncle John said. "But the old Fugitive
Slave Law was enacted in 1793 . . . "

"So long ago!" Wendell was astonished.

"That's the point, Nephew. Then slavery was common.
Boston people had slaves . . ."

"Here?" Wendell could hardly believe Uncle John was
not joking. But he looked serious.

"Of course. Maine and New Hampshire — all New England had slaves. There was little if any feeling against the
custom. They were mostly house servants up here and well
enough treated, except they had no freedom. The law you
ask about ordered that if a fugitive slave, a runaway, was caught
he should be returned to his owner. It seemed right then, for

slaves were property. If my horse was stolen and found, you'd expect it to be returned? That's the way they figured." Wendell was silent, thinking.

Uncle John was still telling of Dana and the arguments when suddenly he said, "There's my man now. Hop out, Wendell. See you soon." Wendell turned and walked home, thinking so hard he failed to look for new ships down the bay.

The case was lost. Newspapers raved or gloated, according to their ideas. Citizens argued; boys in the schoolyard relayed what they heard at home. Wendell was more puzzled than ever before in his life. Two laws: a slave must be returned; a slave could not be sold in Boston. And because of those, it seemed, Anthony Burns' owner was allowed to take him home.

The sheriff hid the rattling irons as they drove Burns to the ship; he wanted no mob scene like the day Thomas Simms was returned. Sullenly, people watched the cart pass. Had a leader been at hand . . . but no one led. On the ship, once it was out in the harbor, Burns was manacled, and his martyrdom began.

Most people forget easily. At school final examinations began. And soon the city was plunged into distress with a terrible epidemic of yellow fever. Illness and death struck seemingly at random. All who could left the city.

The Holmes family had often visited the farm near Pittsfield, a place of several hundred acres that had belonged to Judge Wendell and was given by him to his daughter, Wendell's grandmother. Dr. Holmes bustled them off in a hurry to this safe and distant retreat.

Wendell was glad to go to the country. He loved the woods and the river; the view toward Greylock, the great mountain off to the northeast. He liked hours alone; he needed to think.

Mornings there were chores — feeding chickens, tending garden, picking berries in their season. Afternoons belonged to him. He took a book — there was a good library in the house — and climbed high in some tree to read. He chose different trees so that Edward and Amelia could not easily find him and beg him to play with them.

The family relaxed from city ways. Dr. Holmes had stayed in Boston, where he was needed in the hospital for his courage and cheer as well as for his skill.

After a few days Grandmother Holmes and Uncle John came to the farm, and that made it all the better. John Holmes never hurried. His asthma made it impossible. He could tell good stories, but they were quiet ones. The brothers were very different men. Wendell knew John would never be famous as his father was though no one had ever mentioned that fact. But many friends liked John the better.

Does one need to be famous? Wendell wondered after a happy afternoon with Uncle John. The question struck him for the first time. His grandfather had written a book. His father had written a poem — many poems and other things. People spoke of Dr. Holmes as famous for original studies in medicine.

What could *I* do? How could one possibly decide?

A few days later Uncle John was restless. The day was so fine! "How's to climb Greylock with me, Wendell?" he asked.

"All the way, Uncle John?"

"Well," Uncle John chuckled, "we'll fudge a bit. We'll drive to the beginning of the trail. I know a man there who'll watch my horse while we climb. We'll take lunch in a knap-sack — want to?"

The trail was beautiful, and as they climbed higher and higher the whole range came into view — mountains, valleys, the river and streams. Wendell had never been all the way up Greylock before. They rested at the top and ate lunch. Uncle John stretched out while Wendell looked around, feeling

at the top of the world. Suddenly there was something he must know.

"Uncle John. Why are laws bad?"

"Eh! What's this?" Uncle John sat up, blinking. "Laws aren't bad. Where did you get that idea?"

"The Fugitive Slave Law. It's bad. People ought not obey a bad law."

"You and I and other Bostonians think it is bad, because we are against slavery. Slaveholders think it is a good law, because it returns their property. But times change, and so does thinking. Perhaps more people will come to be against slavery. Then this law must change too."

"How?"

John Holmes eyed his nephew thoughtfully. "People have to care. It doesn't help to break a law — to disobey. Laws are rules people live by. If a law is no longer right and useful, people must care enough to take it off the books, legally."

"Do they ever?"

"Not as often as they should," Holmes admitted. "People are busy with their own affairs; few think of the law — till it is needed."

"You like being a lawyer, Uncle John?"

"The best." He dropped back onto the mossy ground. "Better think of it when you grow up." That seemed a faraway time.

"I am thinking," Wendell said softly. Uncle John put his cap over his eyes and dozed. He did not notice that the boy's eyes were shining as he looked north to the distant peaks.

Years of Growing

4

Boston Harbor

The first thing Wendell Holmes did after the family returned to Boston was to hunt up his friend Henry Bowditch, climb the hill, and see what was new in the harbor. The sight astonished him.

Across the water, in the McKay shipyards, the largest hull he had ever seen loomed above the sturdy ways.

"Whew! She's a big one!"

Henry grinned. He had watched that huge hull grow.

"It'll be the biggest ship ever built," he boasted. "All Boston's going to turn out for the launching."

"When?" Wendell asked.

"Soon. Father says early October. Let's not watch from the hill, like children, Wendie. Let's go in a boat."

"If I'm allowed," Wendell agreed doubtfully.

That afternoon, as soon as his father came home, Wendell was given absent-minded permission . . . His father was interested in a book he had brought.

"Thought you might like to read this," he remarked as he handed it to Wendell. "I took it out from the Athenaeum for you." This was a private library; Dr. Holmes was a member. Wendell read the title, *Uncle Tom's Cabin.*

"It's not a new book," Dr. Holmes explained. "A Connecticut lady who now lives in Cincinnati wrote it. People are talking about it. You were so interested in Anthony Burns, Wendell, I thought you might like to read this. The tale sounds exaggerated, but I'm told it's all based on facts."

To please his father, Wendell leafed through the pages, his thoughts more on the launching than the book. But he took it upstairs and soon was reading rapidly, fascinated. At his suggestion, Mrs. Holmes read it to Amelia and Edward. Wendell was not surprised when his sister wept about little Eva and Uncle Tom — it was a sad book, but exciting.

School began. Wendell tried to catch up on happenings since spring. Newspapers had columns about Kansas and Nebraska — places too far west to interest him. No personal problem about a slave made headlines, so he laid papers aside.

However, talk at home soon showed Wendell that Kansas and Nebraska were important because they had organized to be territories in the United States. Many families from the South had moved west, taking slaves with them. Other families from the East settled there, too; they wanted no slavery. They knew that if territories allowed slaveholding, soon those territories would be states — slave states. Two new slave states would upset the balance — would that be good for the nation?

A mid-westerner, Stephen A. Douglas, made some powerful speeches on the subject. He said, "Let each area vote and find what the majority want." This sounded fair until one remembered that slaves could not vote; they were property, not people. The will of a majority would not be known.

Even in the Middle West where Douglas lived, men were divided on what was just. A group who were against slavery had a meeting in Michigan following one in Wisconsin; they organized a new anti-slavery party with an old and honored name, Republican. Many Whigs — but not all — turned Republican.

Boston people were divided, too. Arguments left men flushed and angry and altered the opinions of no one. Boston hostesses, like Mrs. Holmes, had a hard time keeping peace at supper parties. New Englanders traditionally respected both property and freedom; if slaves were property, what about freedom? To a great many the problem did not seem simple.

One day Wendell read a piece in the newspaper, a letter from a South Carolinian, that taunted New England about "mill slaves."

"What does that mean, Mother?"

"It refers to mill hands — in Lawrence or Lowell, likely," she said. "People work sixteen hours a day in mills and are paid wages that barely buy enough food to keep them alive."

"They can quit," Wendell said.

"And then how will they eat?" his mother asked.

Wendell stared at her. This thought had not occurred to him.

"That's the reason mill hands are against freeing the

slaves," his mother added sadly. "Most mill workers think that if the slaves were free all would come up here . . ."

"And take mill workers' jobs?" Wendell asked.

"Yes, you see how it is. People consider their interests, not their ideals. Can you blame them?"

It was a relief to have October fourth come, the day of the great launching. For one day, as six years earlier when the water was turned on, people forgot troubles and enjoyed themselves. This day celebrated a personal triumph for the builder, Donald McKay, but his shipyard was in East Boston, and local workers had built the huge wonder. All could rejoice with him.

Wendell, Henry, and two friends crowded into a dory and rowed down the river, angling for a good place among scores of other small craft. Looking back, they saw Beacon Hill was packed with people. Flags waved, and bands played.

At the yards men scrambled along the ways, knocking out blocks, greasing timbers.

On the stroke of twelve, cannon boomed. A band played "Hail Columbia." The great hull stirred and fifty thousand people held their breath as Captain Gifford shouted, "I christen you *The Great Republic!*" He smashed a bottle of pure water from Cochituate against her as the hull slid down, down — and with a mighty splash settled on the bay.

The boys lingered, enjoying the hazards of crowded waters, eating lunch they had brought. They saw the new ship maneuvered into position at the yards. Reluctantly they turned for home in the early twilight.

Later Wendell was saddened to read in the newspaper that the great ship had burned at the wharf, in New York, on the eve of her maiden voyage. A tragic ending to a day that had stirred Boston's pride in her shipyards.

Months and years passed.

National tension grew worse. But no dramatic incident, like the plight of Anthony Burns, challenged Wendell's interest. He continued to grow steadily; he was more than six feet tall, a fair student, a constant reader and, in his father's opinion, little credit to the family.

A few days before Wendell's sixteenth birthday, James Buchanan was inaugurated president, March 4, 1857. Buchanan had lived abroad for three years as United States Ambassador to England. He had not had to take a stand on domestic problems. No one knew just what his opinions were, so both North and South hoped for his support.

Two days after the inauguration, Chief Justice Taney of the United States Supreme Court, the highest tribunal in the nation, announced the Court's decision on the Dred Scott case that had been in various courts for some time. The court had decided that Dred Scott was property; he could be sold and taken anywhere.

Like a flash fire, excitement flared over the nation.

Boston people had been slow to take an interest in this case. Wendell had not followed it at all. Now he read the story.

The Negro, Dred Scott, had belonged to an army surgeon in Missouri, a "slave state." The surgeon and his household moved to Illinois and then to Minnesota, both "free" states. After two years they moved back to Missouri. Scott could have stayed north; he was free. But he liked the surgeon and was needed; he thought his freedom was secure. He returned with the family.

The surgeon died quite soon, and Scott sued to establish the fact that he was free (because of the two years away) and his return to Missouri was by choice. Before the case was tried, Scott was sold to a New Yorker and taken east.

Now Scott's problem concerned two states. Appeal was made to the United States Supreme Court; friends were confident he would be declared a free man. The adverse decision astonished most citizens whatever their opinions. Talk in the Holmes household was a fair sample of talk in hundreds of Northern families.

"That is a final blow to the spirit of the Missouri Compromise that has kept peace for thirty-five years!" an excited guest exclaimed.

"What did you expect?"

"Nine judges, seven of them Democrats, five from the South, one Republican, one Whig . . ."

"We ought to wait and read the opinion," Dr. Holmes suggested mildly. "It will come out in a day or two."

"Maybe you'll read it, Doctor. You studied some law. But for me the vote tells the story. Slavery is now a political issue. The time is coming when we shall have to fight it out."

"End slavery or the Union!" another said loudly.

"There you have it — in a sentence!"

Wendell, sitting at his mother's end of the table, thrilled with the excitement of their talk. He listened carefully, knowing he would argue with the boys at school the next day.

But the boys were quarrelsome. The words "Traitor!" "Abolitionist!" were tossed about with reckless drama. After school Wendell walked to Cambridge to talk with his grand-mother.

"Was it like this before the Revolutionary War?" he asked.

"Exactly," she agreed, pleased with his thinking. "People go along with what they are used to; they argue for what they already think. It takes courage to re-think, to change your mind, Wendell. That's the reason so many old-fashioned laws hang on, like that one on runaway slaves."

"How is school?" she asked after more talk. "You'll be coming to college this fall?"

Wendell nodded, eating pie. Harvard College was right around the corner from her house; nothing to get excited about. He was in his last year at Dixwell's Latin School. College was next.

Buchanan's lack of a firm stand, the Supreme Court decision, and other events did not help the nation. That summer of 1857 a depression, like a blight, covered the country. Too many railroads and factories had been built with money too easily borrowed from insecure banks — the whole shaky structure collapsed. Factories closed. Dividends stopped. Thousands were out of work and hungry.

Many changed plans; moved west or went through Sault Ste. Marie to the rich lands of the northwest.

The Holmes family had always been thrifty, not given to luxury. Dr. Holmes' investments in railroads paid no dividends, but he earned a good living. Wendell would go to college as had long been planned.

On a crisp early fall day Wendell, carrying a heavy bag

packed with his things, climbed aboard the Cambridge bus
and paid his five-cent fare. The driver cracked his long whip,
the four big horses dashed across the bridge, the bus bounced
over cobblestone streets and jerked to a stop in Harvard Square.

The scene was familiar — elm trees, one three-story building with a store on the first floor, the Fairbanks scales over
there with two loads of hay being weighed in before selling.
The long hitch rail crowded with saddle horses and teams
showed it was a busy day — harvest time and the opening of
college.

Wendell turned away, found the boarding house where
his father had engaged his room, climbed the stairs, and quickly
unpacked, putting his belongings into the small chest of draw-
ers. He had no thrill of "going away to college," because he

came so often to Cambridge to see his grandmother.

And she was not his only friend in the village.

Some months earlier, Mr. Dixwell had one day asked Wendell to fetch something he had forgotten to bring from home. Wendell graciously went the long way to the house on Garden Street in Cambridge. The door was opened by a pretty dark-haired girl about Wendell's age.

"Father's sent for his books!" she exclaimed laughing. "I'm Fanny Dixwell. Come in while I get the parcel."

Wendell stepped in, marveling, how did she know? Her easy way, saving him explanations, charmed him. And she was so pretty. After that it was truly amazing how many errands Wendell discovered to do for the headmaster! Sometimes he dropped in, without an errand, after seeing his grandmother. He was never in a hurry, either, though he knew he'd be scolded if late to supper.

Now he was in college; he might see Fanny any time. Other youths were strolling by, so he dashed down the stairs and joined them.

"This is a great place for rules," one youth was saying. "Look! No snowballing — in September! No gathering in groups. No swearing. Where do *you* live?" he asked Wendell.

"At Mr. Danforth's." They laughed.

"There you'll have to be up at six, in bed at nine. A written excuse if you attend any but the college church."

"Oh, well . . ." This didn't seem too important to Wendell. He had caught the eye of a tall slender youth beyond the tree. As the complainers moved on, he stepped near.

"I'm Wendell Holmes, freshman," he said.

"And I'm Pen Hallowell of Philadelphia — Norwood Penrose, if you want the whole thing. Freshman, too."

Wendell flushed with pleasure. He had never known a person from Philadelphia. Soon Henry Bowditch came along, and the three talked of classes. There were to be about a hundred freshmen, all studying Latin, Greek, classical literature, and trigonometry.

"In my junior year I'm going to study astronomy and science," Hallowell said. "Though of course I'll get no credits for those."

"Harvard was established for ministers, and they aren't supposed to need such subjects," Wendell said, a little surprised to find himself defending the college. "Things may change."

He might have explained that his father knew Louis Agassiz, the Swiss naturalist now at Harvard, and Asa Gray, the New York botanist, and Benjamin Peirce, gaining renown for his studies of the stars. These men, and others, were slowly to change Harvard College. But it did not occur to Wendell that knowing them was any advantage. He meant to be free of his family. He was in college.

Soon he settled down to regular living. Classes, study, weekends at home where he went to King's Chapel with his family. He didn't work too hard. Gradually he made friends.

In December Hallowell hailed Wendell in the Yard.

"Congratulations!"

"What for?" Wendell exclaimed.

"Haven't you seen it? Your father's done a clever piece

in the first issue of a new magazine — *The Atlantic Monthly.* You should read it."

Uneasily Wendell hurried to the store and got a copy. He tucked it under his arm and hurried to his room to read. There it was — twelve pages. "The Autocrat of the Breakfast Table," by Oliver Wendell Holmes. It was so true it made Wendell remember the marmalade jar; he recognized sentences said at their own table — by his father or guests. How could his father drag it out in print?

When he got home Friday afternoon, his father was surrounded by admiring friends who *liked* being put in a magazine! The little doctor was radiant; his wife proud.

"They're saying I must write more, Son, that I'll make the magazine a success — your father, Wendell!" Dr. Holmes boasted.

"That's fine, Father," Wendell managed to say on his way upstairs. A copy of the *Atlantic* lay on his desk. He read the twelve pages again, trying to understand why his father wrote them. The thing was lively, real — but how could he?

Giving it up, Wendell put the magazine in a drawer, under a pile of socks, and went down the back stairs for some supper.

Weeks passed and every month a fresh article made a stir in Boston. Wendell went less often to see his grandmother — she was sure to be reading the latest *Atlantic.* Instead he dropped in at the Dixwells.' Other youths were there, and girls. Fanny made him feel comfortable and clever — a nice feeling he had not had for some time.

In the late spring the freshmen class was shocked by a

new ruling. No longer was class time to be used for final quizzes to find if students had read their lessons. All were to be examined at once, in writing.

"We'll have to know everything!" a student wailed.

"Let's refuse to take such things!"

"Just how will you do that?" An unanswerable question. So, near the end of the term, classes nervously assembled, quill pens sharpened. Blank books, bound in blue, were passed out. Professors tramped the aisles, proctoring, while students wrote or chewed fingernails and wished they had studied.

The bell rang. Books were collected — and the first final written exams at Harvard ended. Wendell found later that he stood about quarter way down in his class — on the whole, better than he had expected.

Senior
Year

Massachusetts Hall—Harvard

The Holmes family stayed in Boston that summer after Wendell's freshman year at Harvard. They were to move to a house on Charles Street; the boys had a boat they had painted vivid green and named the *Green Dory*. Amelia and her mother enjoyed city activities, and Dr. Holmes had extra work at the hospital. And the Regatta was set for mid-June.

At this time Harvard had no athletic program. If students wanted exercise they used Indian clubs or dumbbells. Or walked. Wendell liked to walk. A young tutor in mathematics named Charles Eliot preferred to row. He organized a Harvard Boat Club, and they acquired a boat big enough for six oarsmen. Daily they practiced on the river and Back Bay, and students took to watching and guessing racing prospects.

On June 19 this crew was to race six other boats in a Boston Regatta. A crowd of watchers turned out early.

Within an hour of the start Tutor Eliot eyed the wide stretch of water between shores.

"How can they tell who is winning?" Eliot asked. "All look
so alike at a distance."

"You've got a point," Captain Crowninshield agreed. "But
it's too late to do anything about that."

"No, we've time." Eliot tucked his watch into his pocket.
"Come with me. Maybe Harvey's store will have some insignia."

Crowninshield saw nothing suitable, but Eliot found six
China silk scarfs of brilliant crimson.

"These will do," he said, buying quickly. "We'll tie these around our heads — people can't miss us!"

The oarsmen liked the idea. They put on the bright scarfs — and won the race. The scarfs, and the color, were counted a lucky omen and were used by the Boat Club in other races. Later, as new sports were introduced, each team wore something crimson, and it became the official color for the college.

The move to the Charles Street home was a pleasant change for the Holmes family. The Back Bay was not yet filled in. Tidal water lapped the garden walls of places on the up-river side of Charles Street. Often Wendell and a friend rowed up river, tied the boat, and then tramped for hours exploring strange woods and byroads.

By the time college opened that fall, streetcars were running to Cambridge by the West Boston Bridge — a much easier ride than the buses which had jolted over the cobblestones.

"Come winter," the driver remarked as he took Wendell's fare, "we'll have a mess of straw on the floor here — to keep your feet warm. These modern improvements are fine, aren't they, son?" Wendell grinned and agreed. He was happy to be getting back to college.

Courses would be much the same as before. But Wendell had been reading good books through the summer. He would enjoy talking things over with college friends. The last week of vacation he had discovered Plato's *Republic* and begun to read it, with a pleasant feeling of superiority. He'd not heard anyone at college mention reading Plato.

On an afternoon when he had no class, Wendell chanced to think of Mr. Emerson — why not walk out and call upon him? Ralph Waldo Emerson, the philosopher of Concord, was a friend of Dr. Holmes; Wendell had heard him talk brilliantly on religion, philosophy, or other topics. He always made Wendell feel awake, grownup.

The day was sunny, the trees barely touched with gold. Wendell enjoyed the long walk.

Mr. Emerson remembered him and made him welcome in

the study, a comfortable room with a wide bay window. A handsome harp stood in the bay. A window was open. Now and then a curtain fluttered and stirred the harp strings to gentle music, like a chord played by an unseen hand. On a table by an easy chair was an attractive blue bowl piled with early yellow apples.

"Help yourself, Wendell." Mr. Emerson gestured toward the apples. "That tree has done well this year." For a while they ate in sociable silence, pleasing to Wendell.

"What are you reading now?" Emerson asked soon.

Wendell launched into talk about Plato. He felt that he talked well. Mr. Emerson listened with flattering attention — a question now and then kept Wendell talking. The striking of the hall clock warned of passing time; Wendell reluctantly tore himself away pleased with an invitation from the great man to come again.

Striding home through afternoon shadows Wendell felt inspired. Surely the life of a scholar or philosopher was delightful. How bright did one have to be? Thought of his indifferent marks gave him pause. He knew Mr. Emerson had a brilliant mind; Dr. Holmes had spoken of it. One had to be bright to be a lawyer, too. A fleeting recollection of Uncle John and the hour on Greylock Mountain went through his mind. It would seem one must be clever to be anything, and Wendell seldom felt clever. He hurried his pace, remembering supper.

That year he wrote a theme on "Books" that was published in the *Harvard Magazine*. Dr. Holmes read it.

"Sophomoric drivel," he remarked and tossed the magazine aside.

Dr. Holmes was having a brilliant success as an author. A group of his *Atlantic* essays had been published as a book. The monthly essays continued with growing popularity. Now he was writing a novel to be called *Elsie Venner*. He loved his work and took a frank pleasure in his success.

Months, a year went by with the same daily round.

Towards Christmas of his junior year, Wendell chanced to come across his Plato. He read it again and was astonished to find that he enjoyed it. He wished he had a complete set of Plato and was given the books for Christmas.

He spent most of the midyear vacation up in his room overlooking the Charles River, reading those books and writing a paper that he decided was excellent.

At his first opportunity he took it out to Concord to Mr. Emerson.

The great man welcomed him and sat down to read the paper. Wendell could hardly contain his impatience as sheet after sheet dropped to the floor.

When the reading ended Mr. Emerson gathered up the sheets neatly and handed the paper to Wendell.

"When you know something about Plato, you will write a paper worth reading," he said, kindly.

Wendell stared. He could hardly say thank you and goodby. He failed to notice that Mr. Emerson asked him to come again soon. Back in his room he tore the paper into shreds and tossed the stuff into the fireplace. Head on his arms, he sat at his desk a long time, deeply discouraged.

A week later he chanced to run into Mr. Emerson in the parlor, at home. The philosopher reached out a hand.

"Are you and Plato getting acquainted?" he asked. His eyes were interested, kind.

Wendell managed to mutter something, he didn't know what. Then he rushed up to his room, got out Plato and began to read. Back in Cambridge, he read every possible minute. For the first time in his life, he did not read for pleasure. He challenged himself to *think*. What did this sentence really mean? Did he, Wendell Holmes, believe that idea?

He began to drive himself to work, day and night. His professors noticed a change in him. His eyes, his expression, were alert. Soon he began another paper on Plato.

At the end of his junior year he stood thirteen in his class. His parents were pleased. They cared more about his standing than about his membership in Hasty Pudding or other good clubs, and his editorship of a college magazine. Now he might be a Phi Beta, like his father and grandfather.

"Glad to see you are bringing up your work, Wendell," Dr. Holmes commented. "Edward stands at the *top* of his class at Dixwell's Latin school. It's time you improved."

"Good for you, Neddy," Wendell said, with real pride in his brother. But he wondered — need brothers always be compared? Edward and I are entirely different people. Somehow the glow of achievement dimmed.

Wendell spent the summer of 1860 doggedly working on

two projects; catching up on politics and rewriting his Plato article. He had suddenly decided to try again and to submit it in the *Harvard Quarterly* contest for the best article written by an undergraduate. In the meantime, politics proved absorbing.

Not all Bostonians were Abolitionists — the nation hardly realized that yet. Mill owners had to have cotton; planters said the cotton crop required slaves. Some of the worst fights on slavery were in mill towns where fear made bad tempers.

The Holmes family and most of their friends were Republicans, but that did not mean that all favored the party's candidate, Abraham Lincoln.

"I can't see how he got the nomination!" men told each other. "A nonentity from the West!"

"I know how he got it," Dr. Holmes said firmly — and when Dr. Holmes spoke everyone listened. "Seward couldn't keep his mouth shut. Seward kept arguing against slavery. Lincoln had sense. He talks about the Union."

"But he'll never get elected — straddling that way."

"Lincoln doesn't straddle — can't you be fair to the man?" Dr. Holmes exclaimed. "Lincoln's against slavery in new territories. That will keep it from growing. He is for protection of American industry — that will help the East. He favors giving free public land to people who will actually move out and settle in the West. The Republican party stands back of all that. Let slavery in the South alone for now."

"Planters know what will happen if Republicans get in," a red-faced mill owner cried. "Slavery will go! The South will secede if Lincoln should be elected — but he won't, not he!"

Back in college for his senior year, Wendell found political discussions even sharper than in Boston. Many Harvard students were Republicans and for Lincoln, but there were scores of Southerners there, too. Debates in clubs and parades on the streets ended in long discussions. It was hard to settle down to work.

As editor of the *Harvard Magazine,* Wendell wrote an article on art that brought some praise. The essay on Plato was published in the October number of the *Quarterly.* Wendell picked up the first copy of the *Quarterly* and a copy of the other magazine and hurried over to Garden Street to show them to Fanny. She was as excited as he hoped she would be. She curled up on a sofa and read both straight through.

"The art essay is the better," she announced. "I didn't know you cared about art, Wendell."

"Didn't I tell you?" he flushed as always when he talked about himself. "I took etching tools to the farm with me, one summer. I learned that I could not draw. But I liked trying."

Fanny gave him tea and praise. He was glad he had come.

The article on Plato won the annual prize, and Wendell had his moment of glory. Fanny still liked the art essay better; she was an independent girl, and Wendell liked that.

Wendell, at nineteen and a half, could not vote. But even without him, Abraham Lincoln was elected president. He got only about forty percent of the popular vote, but his electoral vote was secure.

A month later South Carolina seceded as predicted; Buchanan did nothing as Mississippi, Florida, Alabama, Georgia, and Texas followed. It almost seemed as though they were daring Buchanan to do something! And then, as March drew near, it was too late. Feeling was so intense that it was a relief when newspapers announced the president-elect's safe arrival in Washington and his inauguration without bloodshed.

Through March men in uniforms were in Cambridge — and no longer a surprise. Youths and older men, too, bought copies of the standard manual of arms and studied hard.

One stormy day Hallowell appeared at the door of Wendell's room — in uniform. On the stairway half a dozen classmates trailed behind him. They came in; they sat on the bed, the two chairs, the floor. Hallowell leaned against Wendell's desk, enjoying their surprise.

"Don't you want to graduate?" they asked him.

"I'd thought I did," he admitted. "But after all, a diploma is only a thing. My country needs me."

"Don't give that 'my country' to me," a student said. "You know your country about as far as Philadelphia . . ."

"Wait a minute," Wendell protested. "His country is his country. He can care for what he has not seen."

"I don't. What do any of us know about the United States? Less than we know about Athens. Or Rome."

"Or even London," another broke in. "We've had a classical education, we have. I don't intend to set myself up as a target for geography that I do not know."

"*My* country isn't geography," Wendell said quietly. "My country is an idea."

His classmates looked at him curiously. Wendell Holmes wasn't given to speaking in that tone. They were silent as he went on:

"My country is all the men and women who have made it. My great grandfather, Captain Holmes, and my grandfather Abiel, who wrote it down so we would know. It's my own grandfathers, Judge Wendell and Judge Jackson — and all of *your* forefathers, too. My country is their ideal of freedom and justice and . . ." Suddenly he stopped. I'm making a fool of myself just as my father said I would, he thought.

"I just mean, Pen, I like your uniform. I'm glad you came to let me know you have enlisted."

Early in April, President Lincoln ordered supplies sent to Fort Sumter, in Charleston's beautiful harbor. Three days later the Confederates bombed that fort.

On the fifteenth, the President called for 75,000 volunteers to save the Union. Massachusetts was ready and promptly sent her quota. With flag-waving and songs people bade the volunteers Godspeed. No one expected the war to last long enough to amount to much but thoughtful citizens felt a chill under the surface. War. There had not been a war for so long that few remembered what it was like.

Nine days after the President's call, Wendell Holmes joined the 4th Battalion of the Massachusetts Volunteer Militia to serve on guard duty without pay. This was the unit Hallowell had joined. Other classmates signed on with Wendell. The next day they went to the Armory and put on uniforms — light blue Zouave trousers, dark tunic, red sash.

"Very nice on you," a voice remarked. Wendell turned to see his father standing beside him. He had come to the Armory to see them off for Fort Independence, down the Bay.

His father had the thoughtful, observing look Wendell knew so well. Has he come so he can write about us for the magazine? Wendell thought he could not bear that.

Then, with a sudden change of mood, he was remorseful. His friends were thrilled that the famous Dr. Holmes had come to see them. They thought Wendell was lucky to have such a father. They crowded around the little man. They laughed at his jokes. They were proud to be with the most popular wit in Boston.

Wendell, looking down from his six feet three, felt an unexpected tenderness, a deep affection. When his father turned to leave he said, "Thank you for coming, Father. It was good of you." And he felt better than he had for a long time.

In His Country's Service

6

Union Soldiers Parade

Fort Independence, on an island in Boston Bay, was a familiar place to Wendell Holmes; he had picnicked on its beach. Now, as a soldier, he diligently scanned the horizon for the armed ships with Confederate flags that Boston people expected. The volunteers were resolved to fight bravely to protect the city.

But no such ships appeared. Instead, pretty girls — well chaperoned, of course — came out with hampers of delicious food. These patriotic excursions had much glamor and for the soldiers were a change from hours of training.

On the first day of May, Private Holmes wrote home asking for food; he wanted lots of butter and meat and olives. And a carpetbag to hold his belongings. And handkerchiefs — he had a fearful cold. His hair had been cut — "jail style." He sent a sketch showing clipped hair, long nose and a pipe emitting much smoke.

Henry Abbott, a friend of Wendell's of the class of 1860,

was at the fort. Hallowell, Holmes, and others of '61 had bravely
given up diplomas for war. But as it turned out, the sacrifice
was not needed. They did not even need to give up final
examinations — a disconcerting bit of information that came
to them late in May. They sent for books and studied hard to
make up for lost time.

Pen Hallowell had been elected class orator; now he had
to write the oration. Wendell was class poet — an honor he
did not like because he thought it merely meant he was his
father's son. Most of the years since Dr. Holmes graduated
in 1829 he had been poet of his class. But Wendell felt he could
not honorably resign at the last minute. He must write something.

As May ended, soldiers were withdrawn from the fort; the
4th battalion returned to Boston on a steamboat. Bands played,
and friends were waiting at the wharf.

Belated examinations were in June. The soldier students
had expected to be victors in the South by then. The changed
events seemed incredible. Wendell dashed off a poem of three
stanzas; it would have to do.

Class Day was celebrated in the traditional way. Scores
of charming girls in swirling frocks wandered under the elms of
Harvard Yard with dignified graduates and envious underclass-
men. To his surprise, Wendell saw that Amelia, now seventeen,
was pretty and popular. She could chat and make people laugh
as easily as her father did.

The discovery made Wendell notice Fanny Dixwell —
why, she was pretty, too! He had not thought of this before;

he'd just known that he liked her. Now he watched the crowd
of young men around her and then hastily joined the group.
Imagine! Competing for Fanny! She had always been waiting
when he wanted her.

But for the occasional flash of a uniform under a black
scholastic robe one could forget war — for the moment. Though
here and there small groups gathered to discuss the President's

call for volunteers to serve three years — very different from three months.

Pen Hallowell gave his oration, and Wendell Holmes read his poem. His family, sitting on a front row, applauded loudly with the others. Many in the audience looked knowingly at Dr. Holmes and whispered, "Like father, like son." Dr. Holmes smiled and bowed, knowing some of the applause was for him.

Wendell had not saved his scribbled poem, but a reporter defeated his desire for oblivion. The poem was printed in the newspaper the next day . . . "Dr. Holmes, the famous poet, was proud of his son," the piece said.

Class Day ended with the circles around an elm tree in the Yard — freshmen in the outer ring, sophomores next, then juniors, and the eighty-one seniors closest to the tree. It was all sentimental and thrilling, the more so because of the dangers of war, looming ahead.

Wendell Holmes, like his classmates, had been asked to write his autobiography. These papers were bound as a permanent class record. His was short and factual; he mentioned the three families — Olivers, Wendells, Holmeses, and added his maternal grandfather, Judge Jackson. These men, and the devoted women they married, had been in his thoughts all spring. Each had worked to build the nation; their high ideals seemed very real to him.

He had never worked for a living, he wrote; had been a student except for brief military service. He told of his art essay and the prize for the Plato paper.

"At present I am trying for a commission in one of the

Massachusetts Regiments (he wrote) and hope to go South before very long. If I survive the war I expect to study law as my profession at least for a starting point."

The paper was signed "O. W. Holmes, Jr., July 2nd, 1861." As an afterthought he wrote a penciled note:

("N. B. I may add that I don't believe in gushing much in these College Biog's and think a dry statement much fitter. Also I am too busy to say more if I would.)"

With college over, Wendell devoted his time to getting into service. His cousin, Harry Lee, an enlistment officer, had a suggestion.

"A Harvard company is forming," he told Wendell; "well, it has nothing actually to do with the college. But a lot of Harvard men have signed up for it. I'll try to get you a commission in it."

"I'd like to go soon," Wendell said, much pleased. "I can't seem to settle down to anything." He hurried home, tidied his room, and cleared out college papers. He nearly drove his mother and sister wild dashing hopefully down the stairs every time the door knocker sounded.

The commission came the tenth of July. He was a First Lieutenant in Company A of the 20th Regiment of Massachusetts Volunteers — "for three years of service." He was ordered at once to Camp Massasoit, a few miles from Boston.

On arrival there he found that enlistments were coming in slowly — to sign for three years was more serious than three months; most citizens thought three-years' enlistment was ridiculous.

The nation had changed so rapidly and so importantly through the 1850's that few, either in the North or the South, realized what had happened.

The discovery of gold had drawn people west. The building of a canal and locks to bypass the dangerous rapids at Sault Ste. Marie made it possible to bring iron ore, discovered a decade earlier, to furnaces in the coal regions near the Great Lakes. The North would have plenty of iron.

This same canal allowed access to vast fertile plains in the northwest, and improved plows and reapers made large crops possible. The North would have plenty of wheat. Timber to build homes and factories was coming down, too. The South had cotton to send to northern mills.

But to enjoy this budding prosperity the nation must stay whole. Some, like Lincoln, saw the need of wholeness. They wanted to free the slaves — but the wholeness, union for all the people, must come first. Those who felt this were dedicated to the dream, as were the soldiers in the Revolutionary War long before.

Lieutenant Holmes had been at camp four weeks before the company was full enough to be mustered into federal service. Even then they had no marching orders.

Dr. and Mrs. Holmes drove out to visit their son. Harry Lee came with them to see how the men handled the handsome Enfield rifles the governor had wangled for them. A group of patriotic Boston ladies presented a beautiful white silk banner they had made as the standard for the 20th.

It was a gala day, but official and serious. Wendell missed

the pretty girls who had come to Fort Independence.

Marching orders finally came, and on September fourth the regiment was on its way. They went to New York where they marched in a parade. They shipped to Philadelphia, and via Baltimore, came to Washington on the seventh.

Until he looked into strange crowds in New York, Wendell had not known how he missed the anticipated parade by the Common, the waving of friends, the smiling, familiar faces. His family did not know he had gone until they read in the newspapers that the 20th was in Washington.

"But Wendell will write," Amelia said to comfort them.

"Will he?" Dr. Holmes doubted.

"Will he have time?" Mrs. Holmes added.

On the 8th he wrote from Camp Kalorama on Georgetown Heights, and he appeared to be in good spirits in spite of the tedious journey. His carpetbag was invaluable because his trunk had been bashed. Their possessions were in a mess, but the officers were organizing a new system: one mule-drawn truck for each company so men could get at their things. No fighting seemed near as they were reserves.

Three days later he wrote his mother a long affectionate letter. They had moved. He had a plain view of the unfinished Capitol — a beautiful sight. Officers had to buy their own food; sometimes it was fair, often very bad. He ended with words of deep affection:

"I love you just as much as if I talked with my mouth. God bless daddy too and love to the babbies . . ."

His mother cherished that letter; Wendell wrote more

affectionately than he talked, she thought. Amelia and Edward fussed about being called "babbies," but at school they boasted about their soldier brother.

There was little chance to enjoy the view of the Capitol because the regiment moved on twice, ending at Camp Benton by Edwards Ferry on the Potomac River. From there Wendell wrote a long letter; things were looking "like Biz," he thought. They camped in a grove, by the river; and across, not more than a mile away, they glimpsed rebel soldiers. Occasionally one of their own sentinels "stopped a bullet." Soldier lingo sounded unlike Wendell. A small map he enclosed was very puzzling to his family.

"We must write to Wendell," his mother said, after the letter had been reread at supper. "He begs for letters. Some seem to have missed him. We must allow for that."

Dr. Holmes went directly to his desk to write.

September ended. With October the maples and gumwood trees turned gold and crimson. On long nights of duty Wendell thought about war — it seemed different from what he had expected. There was far too much time for thinking, yet he found it hard to remember ideals that made him enlist in the army.

Those men on Ball's Bluff across the river — were they fighting for what seemed good and important, too? Did they really believe what he had read about "the Southern point of view?" Likely they did, or they wouldn't be there.

On a Sunday, Colonel Palfrey conducted a service of worship. As Wendell sat on a log in a grove of maples his thoughts turned homeward. Father, mother, sister, brother would be hearing words such as these; they would be in the family pew at King's Chapel. Did they miss him?

In thought he followed them home, through dinner and the afternoon. Soon Wendell was thinking about God. Did God watch over a battle? Did a soldier pray and find help? Did . . .

Suddenly a bugle sounded the call to arms. Wendell ran to his station. Men hurried from tents, the woods, the river bank. This was their first call to battle.

It took all night to move the 20th in four leaky scows across to an island and then to the Virginia shore. At dawn Lieutenant Holmes' company lay in tall grass eyeing the woods. The enemy hid there, they were told.

A command came. Company A rose and fired toward the woods. They ran toward the grove, cocking rifles, aiming as they ran. Wendell was out in front waving his men on when a spent bullet hit him in the stomach. Winded, he dropped to his knees.

"Better go to the rear, Lieutenant," a Colonel said as he ran by. But Wendell did not want to go to the rear.

He staggered to his feet. He found that he could still breathe.

The rebels were yelling — the sound was as terrifying as he had been told it would be. Wendell felt a curious tingle as he swayed, getting balance. Then he ran, waving his sword, shouting encouragement to his men. The fighting ahead was hand to hand, he saw.

Suddenly, as he ran, a bullet hit him squarely in the chest, a little left of center. He toppled over, vomiting blood, and then lay still. Pain spread over him; he lost consciousness.

Wendell had no knowledge of the battle raging around him; he didn't know that later a sergeant dragged him out of the way. Or that someone carried him down the bluff to the river.

"You can't get him in the scow; it's full."

"Try this little boat . . ."

Words ran through Wendell's mind. "Take the others first." Did he say them? Or only think them? He didn't know.

Shrill screams roused him. The scow, packed with wounded men, tipped over and sank. Every man drowned. No preparations had been made for retreat. Now everything was confused.

Somehow Holmes was got across the island, across the second stretch of water. The men made a chair and carried him to a temporary field hospital in the woods. The floor was slippery with blood — the sights around him were so shocking that he closed his eyes.

Wendell had carried from home a small bottle of laudanum, a drug to deaden pain. He was about to reach for it when he heard a new voice; an army surgeon was bending over him.

"Tell me the truth," Wendell begged. "Will I get over this?"

The surgeon studied the wound. He picked a bit of cloth from it. "Well, you have a chance. Yes, a chance."

A chance. Wendell longed to be brave. But the scene blurred. He had fainted.

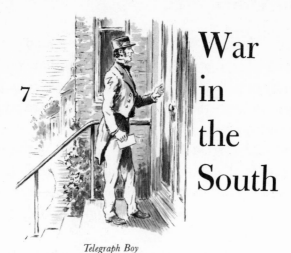

War in the South

7

Telegraph Boy

While Lieutenant Holmes and other wounded soldiers lay bleeding, telegraph wires carried north the shocking news of defeat at Ball's Bluff. Newspapers had no details, just the bitter facts of defeat and casualties.

In the Holmes household, as in hundreds of others, white-faced women went about their duties, silent, tense. Men searched for comfort and found none. Not knowing whether a loved one was alive was worse than anything — no, worse than *almost* anything!

Then a telegram came from Cousin Harry Lee, who had rushed south to get information. Wendell was wounded in the chest but was doing well as could be expected. Pen Hallowell was taking him to Philadelphia.

Five days passed before newspapers had a full account of that battle. The whole affair was a mistake; no attack should have been made at Ball's Bluff. Fresh troops of the Confederate army had surrounded Union troops wearied by a night's task of crossing the wide river. A thousand — one *thousand* — Union men were killed, wounded or missing. This frightful calamity brought no gain of any kind — none!

Suffering, death, anxiety — all useless. "A mistake." How could one endure that, citizens asked themselves.

Dr. Holmes hopefully continued to read the newspapers, and five days later his search was rewarded.

"Look!" he cried. "Here's his name! 'O. W. Holmes. Company A. 24. Law student; wounded in abdomen.' "

"Can that be Wendell?" Mrs. Holmes bent over her husband's shoulder to read for herself. "Wendell is not a law student. He is twenty, not twenty-four. Harry said he was wounded in the chest."

"It's not likely there would be another O. W. Holmes — in Company A." Both parents felt a new alarm.

"I'm going down there and get the truth," Dr. Holmes announced. "Nothing I do here is important!"

"Don't talk that way about your work," Mrs. Holmes exclaimed. "Wendell is cared for — Harry will have seen to that. He took nurses with him, remember? Anxious parents milling around will only make more confusion. Have faith and wait."

Reluctantly Dr. Holmes was persuaded.

Definite word came later. Wendell was improving. By a miracle the bullet had gone through his chest, missing heart and lungs. He was on his way to the Hallowells.

Three weeks after the battle Dr. Holmes went to Philadelphia to bring his son home. The doctor was shocked at the first glimpse of Wendell, so pale, so gaunt.

"Can you travel?" he exclaimed.

"Of course, Father; I'm fine now. I want to go home."

Arrangements were made for the journey. Dr. Holmes could hardly wait till the train pulled out, leaving kind friends behind. At the Hallowells Wendell was so quiet and there were a thousand questions Dr. Holmes wanted answered.

"How did it feel, in battle, Wendell?" he began.

"Was the rebel yell frightening?"

"They say bullets 'whiz' — how does that sound?"

Dr. Holmes paused; Wendell had not spoken. The youth lay on turned-back seats; his eyes closed. The effort of boarding the train had left him spent. Dr. Holmes was silent, awed by what war had done to his son.

At home, Wendell lay on his own bed, relaxed. Dr. Bigelow came to examine him, gave soothing medicine, and Wendell slept. Amelia and Edward tiptoed in to see him, and went out, silently.

In the morning Wendell ate breakfast and announced that he was better. In a few days he demanded visitors.

"Where is Fanny?" he asked. "What are Ida and Mary doing? Isn't anyone coming to see me?"

When young people were around him, Wendell talked gaily enough. But he would not speak of battle.

Hours in the darkness he thought of words he had jotted down while in the hospital; words that were for himself, or maybe, someday, for his mother.

He had written of his struggle with the wish to deaden pain with that drug he had carried and his decision that he

should not use it. He had described the sights and smells of the
hospital — more blood and carnage than he could have im-
agined. He had tried to put into words his wonder about death
— what came after? Would he still be O. W. Holmes, Jr.?
What did he believe?

These jottings told nothing of the will to live, because he
knew nothing of this force. Gradually and surely his will to
live was stirred. Thoughts of home and friends brought a
longing to see them. His will to live had given him the courage
to endure the jolting cart, the transfer to a canal boat and to the
home that sheltered him.

While Wendell grew stronger, Dr. and Mrs. Holmes continued their daily work with the Sanitary Commission, a branch
of the Army Medical Corps. Dr. Holmes trained medical aides
and nurses. Mrs. Holmes worked with supplies. The commission equipped hospital ships; sent out drugs, bandages, food,
coffee — anything that was needed and could be obtained.

Everyone read newspapers, searching for victories that did
not come. General McClellan had a gift for delaying action or
acting at the wrong time and place. People criticized Lincoln,
too. Many blamed him for all that went wrong.

With the new year Lieutenant Holmes was recovered and
had orders to do recruiting work in his state. He had come
through battle; this might reassure men who hesitated to enlist.
He had a straightforward manner; his honest gray eyes ap-
pealed. He loved his country and had faith in Lincoln.

"I wish you could see the unfinished Capitol at Washington," he said to one group. "The President is pushing work on it even in war. He has faith that this nation will live. But he needs our help."

Thankfully the family sat down to Wendell's birthday dinner. A twenty-first birthday seemed to call for a party but March 8 that year was a Sunday. The family attended church. After dinner Wendell went to Cambridge to call on his grandmother. Uncle John was there, still unmarried; still devoted to his mother. He teased Wendell about his "many ladies." Wendell enjoyed the teasing and suddenly decided to call on Fanny Dixwell — might as well while he was so near.

On a Monday morning two weeks later, new orders arrived. O. W. Holmes, Jr., was promoted to captain. He was to join his regiment at Hampton, Virginia. He left at once. This time he knew exactly what war was — and he faced it bravely.

Orders were to travel light, so he went by train to Philadelphia where he left his small trunk at the Hallowells. Then he joined his regiment near Washington. He had time for a note to his mother saying that he had arrived and was well.

Two days later the regiment shipped by transport for Hampton. From there they were to march up the Peninsula and capture Richmond.

Rain began almost at once and for weeks the army ate, slept and marched in mud and water. They learned to improvise beds on stilts. They dragged cannon through deep mire. Their blue uniforms were ruined by mud; they were never dry.

Wendell wrote a long letter to his "Dear Parents" . . . "I am

in good spirits though of course I despise the life itself outside of the special circumstances and principles . . ." He enjoyed his friends, Henry Abbott, Pen Hallowell, and Pen's older brother, Edward. He had a cold; the men all had colds from the wetness. He wished for letters.

In April he sent a sketch of Pen and himself huddled under a rain-cover on picket duty. Pen had a beard and a clay pipe, Wendell, his meerschaum.

"Tell Amelia (he wrote) I was delighted with her letter. I

want her to write often; once a week is seldom . . . Tell people to write."

Then they were near the enemy. A letter went to his mother.

"I only write to say all's well and God bless you, dearest."

These nights when he lay awake, cold, wet, often ill with dysentery, his thoughts were of the home that he had once taken for granted. He thought of his gifted father; his mother's devotion; his sister and brother. The strictness of his upbringing now seemed right, for it made life easier. His own self-discipline in service was more rigid than anything he had known at home. Life required rules; he learned that.

In May the regiment was at Yorktown. They shipped up the York and Pamunkey; were marched to the Chickahominy River — and battle.

Newspapers told that the 20th Massachusetts was at Harrison's Landing, on the James River; that they fought in the Seven Days' Battle. There was no victory; only heavy losses on both sides; men were exhausted. The Union Army had not taken Richmond.

"But Father, I don't understand," Amelia said, when her father read that. "Our men are brave. They are *there,* near Richmond." She pointed on the map, which was now kept handy. "Why don't they take Richmond and stop the war?"

Dr. Holmes eyed her anxious face.

"Daughter, wise men are trying to find that answer. For me, I only hope."

The men of the 20th were as puzzled as people at home.

They had no knowledge of various campaigns, east and west. Their strength was spent in a vast effort to keep alive, to follow orders, to find food and get sleep.

On Charles Street the family were never sure that Wendell got their letters. Did he know that his grandmother had died in August? Did he try to write? Was he *alive?*

In September, the 20th was far north in Maryland, near Antietam Creek. Wendell had had a day in Washington where he had got store clothes to replace his ruined uniform. He had eaten a wonderful meal — which made him sick.

Under McClellan they joined in the Maryland campaign to check Lee's invasion of the north. A battle was impending.

Before dawn on the seventeenth Wendell managed to write.

"I don't talk seriously for you all know my last words if I should come to grief. You know my devoted love for you. Why should I say more? It's rank folly pulling a long mug every time one may fight or may be killed. . . . I have lived on the track on which I expect to continue travelling if I get through . . . Deepest love. Love to All — Your Son W.

The battle Wendell had anticipated began before daylight. It appeared to be just another in the now long succession of battles he had shared, except that in the morning he made a dreadful mistake.

His company had marched to the West Woods by way of the Hagerstown Pike. He got them through the woods safely. But in the open he was blinded by smoke-laden mist. He lost all sense of direction — where was the enemy?

One of his men turned and fired, back, the way they'd come.

"You fool!" Captain Holmes shouted. "You're firing at our own men!" He struck the man with the flat of his sword.

As the man toppled over, Holmes heard a shout.

"The enemy are behind us!" The captain had been wrong. Holmes turned to apologize, but there was no time.

The enemy surrounded them.

"Twentieth retire to the right!" an order rang out. The uninjured obeyed in good order, but only a fraction got away safely. Captain Holmes was not among them.

As he had repeated the order, a bullet struck him in the neck. He tottered and fell, bleeding, unconscious. Vaguely he heard a voice. "This man is dying. We must help those who can be saved." And he heard no more.

Fighting forces moved on. The dead and wounded of both sides lay where they fell.

Some time later Captain Leduc, an acquaintance of the Holmes family, chanced to come that way and recognized Holmes. He got a surgeon; had his neck bound up. With a farm lad to help, they got the wounded man to stand, and then walked him to a nearby house. The place was packed with wounded.

"Wendell!" it was Pen Hallowell's voice. "Have you seen Ned?"

"No. I haven't," Holmes managed to reply.

But quickly he felt better. Pen was here. An aide loosened his bloody collar and bound his neck better. The aide's warning to be quiet — a neck wound was dangerous — failed to frighten Holmes. That night, before Ned Hallowell was found, Pen and Wendell and others were loaded into a wagon and taken to Keedysville. When they were off, Captain Leduc telegraphed to Dr. Holmes:

"CAPTAIN HOLMES WOUNDED SHOT THROUGH THE NECK THOUGHT NOT MORTAL AT KEEDYSVILLE. WILLIAM G. LEDUC."

The message got to the house on Charles Street at two o'clock that night. Pounding of the knocker awakened Dr. Holmes. Dazed, he hurried down stairs. The sight of the dreaded yellow envelope unnerved him. He could hardly find the dollar and thirteen cents to pay for the collect message.

The boy dashed off, his hands full of yellow envelopes, as Dr. Holmes opened the thing and read the message.

"Not mortal!" he cried. "What does the man know about a neck — windpipe. Jugular artery. Spine. Nerves.

"Wendell is in danger. I shall set off at once."

This time Mrs. Holmes helped him dress and pack a bag, Edward ran to the corner to hunt a cab. Dr. Holmes just made the four o'clock train to New York. At home, waiting began.

Morning newspapers told of a victory — and more than 20,000 casualties. That battle at Antietam Creek, September 17, 1862, was the bloodiest single day of the Civil War. But the Union Army stopped the northern invasion. They gave the President the victory he had awaited. Now he could announce the Emancipation Proclamation.

This document, already approved by the cabinet, was an-

nounced on the twenty-third. It ordered that slaves in states
that had rebelled against the Union were declared free on the
coming New Year. To many, this Proclamation was as important a paper as the Declaration of Independence.

But wounded soldiers, housed wherever room could be
found, did not have the thrill of knowing this news. Families
awaiting word, as the Holmes family was, found it hard to
rejoice. Where was Wendell? Was he better?

Dr. Holmes went to New York and on to Philadelphia. His
son was not there. Pen had not seen him since Keedysville.
For six days the little doctor searched, following clues by cart,
by wagon, by train.

He was in a hotel in Harrisburg when a message was
handed to him; Wendell was better, was coming by train to
Harrisburg the next day. It was signed by a Mrs. Kennedy.

"Now, who is she?" Dr. Holmes asked the operator. Then
he added, "But no matter. My son is coming." He slept that
night as he had not slept in weeks.

As he went to meet the train he reminded himself, I must
be calm. Wendell hates a fuss. He climbed aboard. Wendell
sat near the door, thin, pale, weary — but alive.

"How are you, Wendell?" the doctor put out his hand.

"How are you, Father?" Wendell said, smiling.

I'm going to get the boy home, the Doctor thought, and
felt a great thankfulness.

"My Hunt for the Captain"

8

Gettysburg Address

At last the long, tedious journey ended. They were home, and Dr. Holmes could turn Wendell over to his mother. That done, he hurried to his study, thrilled with a new idea that had come to him as they traveled.

His whole experience, from the telegram to arrival home, was not unique; thousands of people, both Northerners and Southerners, had loved ones in the army; he had actually seen scores of anxious, harrassed relatives hunting among the dead and wounded — why not write a human interest story about all that? Because of his war work, he had not written anything for the *Atlantic* for some time. The editor would welcome a story — especially this story. He got out paper, sharpened quills, and went to work.

In his third-floor room Wendell's wound healed slowly. And his spirit lagged behind his body in mending. He would not see pretty girls. He wanted no gay talk. Uncle John came to see him, a sad uncle, still mourning his mother.

"You know, Wendell, I thought I could have her many years yet. She was only ninety-three."

Wendell closed his eyes. He could vision his grandmother, alert, interested. He had never thought of her age. But since he last saw her great numbers of young men had died before they had lived. Uncle John should be thankful his mother had had so much of life. But how could one say that?

Mrs. Holmes sent John away. She kept Amelia and Edward out of Wendell's room.

"Can't you see he's tired?" she asked. "It's not just his wound. It's the war — the whole thing."

Suddenly Wendell got up and dressed.

"Why don't my orders come?" he demanded. "The war's not won. I shouldn't be loafing here."

One day his father bustled in, rustling sheets of proofs. "You'll like this, Wendell," he said, beaming.

After his father went downstairs, Wendell picked up the galleys and glanced over several. He dropped them, only to read again with fascination and dismay.

Here, in print, was the story — the *whole* story of his father's search for his son, for himself. There were galleys of it!

Under the title "My Hunt for the Captain," the story began with the arrival of the telegram at two in the morning after the battle of Antietam. Wendell read of the rush for the train, the crossing from New York to New Jersey and another train, the sights on the way . . .

"Father doesn't miss a thing!" Wendell muttered, astonished. "He writes so well." The canal boat passing near the train, moving slowly, "like a blind man, led by a dog." A vivid picture.

Dr. Holmes had bought newspapers in New York. In the train he read of the bloody battle — and did not want to talk to the man in the seat beside him. That moved Wendell. He had never known his father to crave silence; he must indeed have been disturbed.

Wendell read on, learning of the long, disheartening search; he marveled at his father's endurance and cheerfulness. He read

of their meeting on the train and caught his breath in vexation. "How are you, Boy?" "How are you, Dad?"

He never called me "Boy," Wendell protested to himself. I never called him "Dad." Having told so much, why couldn't his father have told that truly?

This small thing suddenly made the whole story unbearable. Wendell's eyes raced through the last paragraphs, sentimental in the popular fashion of the day; thousands would read those lines through a mist of tears.

The strips of proof fell to the floor as Wendell Holmes buried his face in his hands. Something inside him, some inward need of privacy was grievously hurt — a wound worse than any made with a bullet. He loved his father — often he was proud of him. But he could not understand him — less now than ever before.

Orders came the fifteenth of November. The article was to be in the December issue of the *Atlantic*. By then, Wendell would be far away from the approving chatter of delighted readers. He was glad for that.

With Henry Abbott, Captain Holmes went to Falmouth and settled in the bleak headquarters on the Rappahannock. Almost at once he was ill again with dysentery.

He was sent to a hospital tent but had no nursing care. Sounds of battle distressed him. He felt ashamed to be lying in a tent while other men fought. At Fredericksburg he did not know that more men died from illness caused, as his was, by bad food and hard living conditions than died in battle. He was miserable, being "safe!"

When he rejoined his regiment he found the whole feeling changed from the early weeks of the war. The Army of the Potomac was discouraged and sad. Letters seemed to show that the whole nation — both sides — was depressed by the hard realities of a long war. Of an evening at homes in the north, young people gathered around square pianos of gleaming rosewood and sang sorrowful war songs — "Tenting tonight on the old camp ground," "Farewell, mother, you will never see your darling boy again." Tears flowed with a kind of perverse pleasure in the sad songs.

Spirits were so low that the company rejoiced when they were ordered into the town of Fredericksburg and somewhat better shelter. Wendell was given charge of policing, as Provost Marshal — extra work but a change.

Through that miserable late winter the enemy camped near; it was hard to keep the soldiers from fraternizing. Both sides fished under enemy guns. On the sly, they exchanged supplies — a worrisome state of affairs, for who could tell whether some were spies? The officers were relieved when orders came in May, to march.

Their route lay along a plank road under hills known as Marye's Heights — a part of a campaign under General Hooker. As the mist of early dawn cleared, Captain Holmes saw that his company was directly under fire from rebel guns.

"Lie flat!" he shouted as guns blazed. A part of his cape was torn from his uniform. The aim was a bit high but the rebels would get that right by the next round.

"Lie low!" he shouted again and buried his face in his arms.

The next round shot him in the heel leaving him dazed with intense pain. Instantly there came to his mind scenes around hospitals — the gory piles of amputated arms and legs. Now *my* leg is gone, too, he thought. And fainted.

How he got to a hospital was a mystery. For two days army surgeons delayed operating, divided as to whether his foot should be amputated. Then splintered bone was taken out.

"I think we can save the foot," a surgeon said. Holmes said those words over and over, marveling at his good fortune. In a few days he was in Philadelphia; three weeks later he traveled home by himself.

The mood of thankfulness stayed with him. He was pleased with his first caller, John Ropes. John was a practicing lawyer; his younger brother, Henry, was in the 20th, a friend of Wendell's. Wendell set his foot on a chair and settled down to enjoy John's talk — the two men liked each other.

Dr. Bigelow came daily and gradually grew more cheerful about Wendell's foot. He was treating it by a new method; he kept the wound open with a plug of raw carrot, changed daily.

"You had me worried for a while there," he finally admitted to his patient. "The army doctors let the wound close outside. I let it close from the inside first. Makes less pus," he explained with professional pride. "Someday your foot will be as good as new. But it's going to take time. Better admit it and settle down."

Settle down — who could do that while the war was yet to be won? Captain Holmes had not known until after he was at home that the battle in which he was wounded was a Confederate victory. When he learned that he wanted to get back to the field.

The next time John Ropes came he brought with him two books — Wendell had not read a book in months. He enjoyed these so much that Dr. Holmes stopped at the Athenaeum and brought an armful, good books that would stir a man's mind.

Then came news of the battle of Gettysburg, July 1, 2, and 3. Henry Ropes was killed, along with many other friends. Later news got through that Vicksburg had fallen to Grant on July 4—two great Union victories, but at what terrible cost!

Amelia dashed up the stairs with an official envelope.

"Open it quickly, Wendie. But you can't go! You can't even walk yet!" she panted.

It was Captain Holmes' promotion to Lieutenant-Colonel — an empty honor. The 20th was so depleted by casualties it did not need new officers and anyway, as Amelia said, he could not yet return to service.

Spurred by success in two areas, Lincoln decided to increase the army by drafting and push the war to a finish. Draft riots raged in Boston and other cities. Captain Holmes went to Pittsfield and did some recruiting.

In November plans were made to dedicate the cemetery at Gettysburg; soldiers had been buried there, where they fell. The Holmes family had two reasons for watching this event — the friends buried there, and the fact that Boston's popular orator, Edward Everett, was to be the speaker of the day. At the last minute, Abraham Lincoln had been invited to "say a

few words," a courtesy to the President. Newspapers carried
Everett's two-hour speech.

"Good, as he always is," Dr. Holmes decided.

"What did the President have to say?" Mrs. Holmes asked.

"Very little. No one expected him to do well. At least he
spoke briefly. The paper says it was a cold day."

Most people, reading the two speeches, agreed with this.

Friends rallied to make Wendell's convalescence agreeable.
John Gray, a lawyer before he joined the 12th Massachusetts,
was at home and came to see Wendell. Leslie Stephen, of London, visiting in Boston, called on him. Mr. George Shattuck, a
fine trial lawyer, had moved near the Holmes' house on Charles
Street. He invited several young men to see his new library.
Wendell hobbled over and was rewarded by a good time.

The talk turned to whether men knew what they were
fighting for.

"Do they hate each other? Are they so far apart, Holmes?"

"No, they don't hate — at least most of them don't." Holmes
told of the fraternizing near Falmouth.

"They both fight for an ideal they call freedom. It just
happens they see a different angle."

"How is that?" Stephen asked.

"The Union men fight to keep whole — a nation of free
men. The South fights for freedom to leave. They want to go
it alone."

"Sounds simple, the way you put it." Stephen seemed surprised.

"Ideals usually are simple," Holmes said. "But the way to

establish a national ideal often proves to be very bloody."

That evening's talk made Holmes more restless. His orders came in January. He was to be aide to General Wright, on the Rappahannock.

"Good! You'll be safe with a general!" Amelia cried.

"It's Cousin Harry's doing," Mrs. Holmes said. Afterward she remembered that Wendell had said nothing about it being safe. Amelia had not noticed that generals were killed, too. Wendell had six months left of his enlistment — it took only an instant to be killed.

Wendell got off without a fuss — that pleased him. He found what was left of the 20th with the 6th Corps by the Rapidan. Men crowded around him asking what home was like. They couldn't remember, so he tried to tell them.

On Holmes' twenty-third birthday word came that Grant was appointed Lieutenant-General and given command over all Union armies. At his headquarters at Culpeper, Virginia, near where Holmes was, Grant began a thorough reorganization of the Army of the Potomac.

Spring came; trees bloomed in fragrance. One could hardly believe that war existed — until General Wright moved the fight into a horrid maze called the "Wilderness." As they pressed south, men were shot down. Henry Abbott had to be left to die. Holmes thought he could not bear it — but he had to go on.

Suddenly Grant detached three brigades. He sent them north to defend Washington, which was threatened.

Captain Holmes was in Alexandria when word came that

President Lincoln had driven out to welcome the troops. He was coming again the next day, too. If there was fighting, he wanted to see it.

There was plenty of action. Guns blazed. Men were shot down. Holmes looked to the right from the ramparts of Fort Stevens as an officer fell — and beside the fallen man stood the President!

"Get down, you fool!" Holmes hardly recognized his own voice.

The President was absorbed in the firing, but he turned and saw that Captain Holmes had spoken to him! He obeyed.

"I'm glad you know how to speak to a civilian," he said. "I need to be reminded of my own task," and went below.

In the night the rebel army slipped away, carrying a vast amount of provisions. But at least they had gone. Washington was safe.

Later that same month of July, Holmes' three-year enlistment was to end. Rumor said that the 20th might be mustered out — very little was left of it.

"I think I should re-enlist," Holmes remarked to another aide. But he hesitated; he felt too utterly weary to be a good soldier. When the day came, he boarded the train for home.

On the journey he thought of the three train rides he had taken as a wounded soldier — strange how life had repeated itself. The pain, the kindnesses — three times all so alike. Now, he sat alone, staring out blankly.

His father would have found interest in the passing scene. But his father had not served three years in war.

The train jerked to a stop, jarring Wendell's neck; it still hurt at times. People got on. The conductor crunched along the hot, cindery aisle collecting new fares. He eyed the young officer anxiously.

"War does something to 'em — if they live," he said as he punched a ticket. "That young fellow down there — must be six foot tall or more when he stands straight. Look at his faded blue, his tarnished buttons, his stained sash. He's so thin that his hat comes down on his forehead. He'll flesh up some with home cooking. But I don't like the look in his eyes. Sort of haunts a man."

He smiled at the officer, but Holmes did not see him. His thoughts were on his dead comrades; on their families, broken by war. And most of all on the immense task of rebuilding the nation after the war was won.

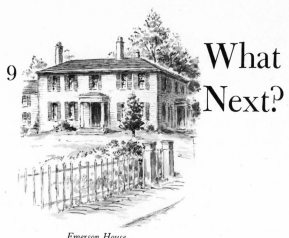

9 What Next?

Emerson House

At home his own friends and family friends called on the returned soldier.

"Victory will come any day, now," several remarked.

"With Grant leading, the South has no chance."

One day several of his father's friends talked freely and in tones of confidence.

"The South could only win by destroying the federal government. They're not strong enough for that," one said.

"They don't expect to win," another added. "They are holding off hoping for a compromise."

"The two sections proved to be more evenly matched than I had expected," an elderly man said to Wendell. "I never thought the war would last three years."

"Both sides have men of courage," Wendell said. "Both are fighting for an ideal they call freedom. The North wants to give the nation a chance — as Lincoln expressed it — 'for the experiment in freedom to prove its worth.' The South fights for freedom to leave a union they no longer want . . ." The young soldier spoke with conviction that came from long discussions on these ideas.

Dr. Holmes stared at his son. The boy was not in the habit of talking so positively among older men.

"Well, you might put it that way," the elderly man admitted. "But factories and furnaces count, too."

"Oh, well. The contest will end soon. Lincoln will be elected. We can count on him to make a just peace."

Talk drifted to other matters. Wendell had the uneasy feeling that he had said too much, and he slipped away, upstairs.

The Class of 1861 held its annual reunion soon after that, and the class poet was expected to write a poem. Wendell wrote something — four verses; but he did not enjoy the occasion. Too many of his friends were absent — dead, or fighting.

In Cambridge he wandered around in the Yard; made some inquiries at the registration office and found that classes were larger than in his time. The North certainly was not using all her manpower.

A loyal crowd gathered on the Common on an August day to see what was left of the once proud 20th Regiment of Massachusetts Volunteers mustered out. Wendell Holmes ended his three years of service with honor and the rank of Lieutenant-Colonel. After the ceremony, friends came to shake his hand. Many he did not know spoke kind words. Then he went home and put on his civilian clothes.

"What are you planning to do next, Son?" Dr. Holmes

asked the question at breakfast the following morning. The query was natural enough. Wendell was surprised it was not asked the day he returned from service. He swallowed a mouthful of porridge and wondered whether to evade or be frank.

"I plan to study law, Father," he said, deciding on frankness.

"*Law!* You'll soon change your mind about that! I tried law and found it utterly stupid." Dr. Holmes' tone implied that the matter was now settled.

"I want to be a lawyer, Father," Wendell said quietly. "A jurist, if I can be. This is no sudden choice. I wrote law as my profession when I enlisted."

"Lawyer. Jurist," Amelia broke in. "What's the difference?"

Dr. Holmes looked up wondering what his son would say.

"Both study law, Amelia," Wendell said. "A lawyer tries cases in court and gives legal advice. A jurist continues study, trying to understand law. He writes and lectures and maybe is a judge."

"Sounds like quibble, quibble to me," Amelia laughed.

"It is," Dr. Holmes said. "Moreover, you'll never gain fame studying law."

"Fame!" Wendell was astonished. "Must I try for fame because you have it, Father? What I want is an interesting life and a chance to earn a living."

"What do you know about earning?" Dr. Holmes exclaimed. "You've never earned a penny!"

Wendell flushed hotly. Already he had felt the yoke of dependence almost intolerable.

"I promise you I shall be on my own as soon as I can . . ."

"Wendell! Don't be silly!" his mother exclaimed. "Your father does not begrudge you the training that is your just due. As for lawyers, Husband, aren't you forgetting John Adams, Thomas Jefferson, and many others?"

"Those men were statesmen." Dr. Holmes could be very stubborn. "Lawyers are little men who sit at desks hunting in big books for details that do not matter.

"Don't misunderstand me, Son. I want you to have all the education you desire. Why not be a scientist? A writer? A teacher? A man can do something in those fields. I take it that you do not choose to study medicine."

The hall clock struck as he said that last word. Dr. Holmes recalled an appointment and hurried away.

Wendell was in no mood for further talk, so he went to his room. He picked up the book he had been reading the night before, but he did not open it. Without really seeing the scene, he looked out over the Charles River, his mind on his father's words.

I might try writing, he thought, not poetry, but other writing. Would my words be worth printing and reading?

Perhaps lecturing would be better. Father said I never could be good at speaking and my neck was too long. He went to the mirror and stretched his neck, testing. In everyday clothes it looked worse than in uniform, he decided. Then he recalled that he had talked to many groups while recruiting. No one had seemed bothered about his neck; he got volunteers. And his mother had said he could do anything he chose to do.

To his surprise he thought of Mr. Emerson. In college he had toyed with the idea of being a philosopher. He had felt inspired on a visit to Concord.

Perhaps Father is right, Wendell thought. He speaks from conviction, not malice. And he tried law. I should talk with Mr. Emerson again. Pleased to have a decision, he gathered up some books that were due at the library and went out.

The day was golden, late summer at its best. Mr. Emerson welcomed his visitor and led him out on the lawn. Chairs were set under the elms; on a table was a pitcher of lemonade and tumblers. Holmes stretched out his long legs, enjoying himself. Mr. Emerson never bustled; he seemed to have plenty of time.

They talked of the war and its outcome; of the many kinds of freedom involved. Mr. Emerson was a student of freedom.

"We fought for freedom — or so we thought," Wendell said. "But I see now that we learned more than a meaning of freedom; we learned faith. A soldier has to have faith that what he is fighting for is right even though he does not understand it; many didn't. A soldier has to have faith in his leaders, too; faith in their skill and understanding — and often he does not feel sure of that either."

Emerson nodded but did not speak.

"It took me a long time, and many battles, to learn faith, Mr. Emerson. But now I know it is as necessary as guns."

The older man put his fingers tip to tip — a favorite gesture. "My generation missed war," he said thoughtfully. "It was counted good fortune. Your generation is given the chance for war experience. When you have had time to ponder, you must pass your ideas on to others. Have you thought of studying philosophy?"

"Yes, I have thought of it," Holmes admitted. His host did not press the point. Talk wandered freely — books, people, ideas. Wendell felt himself expand under this benign influence. He felt uplifted; he could see the whole world.

"This life, this place," he said, "is perfection."

They had not mentioned practical matters, but Wendell knew from his father's comments that Mr. Emerson earned a good living with writing and lecturing.

But on the long way home Wendell wondered; would he be content to sit in a garden, or by a fire, thinking? Could he write steadily? Would his thoughts be worth reading? Surely he needed more training. He came to the bridge over the Charles River and looked down the bay. He turned and looked upriver, too.

Suddenly he thought of Greylock and the view he loved from that mountain. He had been sure of his choice of a profession then. He was sure now. He walked on home, a great peace in his mind and heart.

As he climbed the stairs he heard a sound in his brother's room and knocked on the door.

"When are you going to college, Neddy?" he asked as his brother opened the door. Edward would be a sophomore.

"Oh, the fifth, I think it is. Why?"

"I'll go with you. I'm entering Law School."

"I'm glad," Edward said, proud to be told first. "Where will you room?"

"Oh, at home. It's not fair to ask Father to pay out money when there is plenty of room here. Nickels for car fare won't be much. My room is a good place to study."

"Fanny'll be glad you have decided," Edward said.

Wendell was astonished. He knew Edward had been seeing Fanny's young sister, Susie Dixwell, but why should he think of Fanny in connection with Wendell's career? Would Fanny care? Would she even be interested? Edward watched his brother. Wendell might be smart; but he certainly didn't know much about girls.

"Why don't you go over and tell her now," he suggested casually. "Father said I could have the buggy, but I don't want it for a while. Tell her before your news gets around."

"I believe I will," Wendell said. "Back for supper, Mother," he called as he dashed down the stairs.

On the fifth of September the brothers left for Cambridge. Both wore their best suits. Edward carried a carpetbag with an air of careless sophistication befitting an aged sophomore. Two books were tucked under Wendell's arm and on his face was a look of exaltation. He was beginning his life work.

Wendell registered in a white-pillared brick building called Dane Hall. This name suggested the less than fifty years of history of the Harvard Law School. The first study of law in this college founded to train ministers began in 1815 with one lecture course for which no credit was given. Two years later

a law school was organized. Only graduates were admitted, but so few wanted to attend that requirements were lowered from three years of study to two.

Students laboriously copied legal documents, read books, and listened to a few lectures. They were allowed to attend the county court next door, but few bothered. Six graduated in the first class, and later classes were smaller.

A brilliant and patriotic lawyer, Nathan Dane, became interested in this budding law school. Dane had served in the Continental Congress and had helped to write the charter for

the Northwest Territory. He thought his country needed more
and better lawyers. So in 1829 he gave Harvard $10,000; the
income on this was to pay the salary of a professor of law.

Judge Joseph Story accepted the new position. He was an
associate justice of the United States Supreme Court in Washington, but the federal court did not take all a man's time.
Story could lecture in Cambridge, too. He taught for sixteen
years and kept his interest in the law school still longer.

Soon after the first gift, Dane gave money to build a building for the law school; it was named for him. But these changes,
good as they were, did not make the school grow much; men
learned law in law offices. Dr. Holmes was very angry when
he heard that Wendell had registered.

"If you must study law," he cried, "why not let me get you
a place in an office? I have friends. I am not unknown in Boston."

Amelia, coming down the stairs, giggled. The idea of her
father being unknown was just too ridiculous.

Dr. Holmes reached up and patted her, anger gone.

"I'm just thinking of your own good, Wendell," he said
reasonably. "The law school is where the medical school once
was — beginning. They'll make you copy things; much better
to do your copying in an office where law is in action. The
school has a good library, but I can get you a card for that.
Out there you'd have to listen to lectures for eighteen months
— on philosophy, ethics — I pity you."

"But father, I *like* ethics. I *want* to hear lectures on philosophy." Wendell's strained voice showed his effort to be polite

and fair. "Law is man's effort to live with his fellowmen. Philosophy is a part of law — can't you see?"

Dr. Holmes stared at his tall son. Standing so close, the ten or eleven inches difference in their height was almost painful — does a little man ever *like* a tall, handsome son?

"Really, my dear," Dr. Holmes had turned from Wendell to his wife, "I don't understand our little boy any more. He reads too much; he is confused. I know Harvard. He will get more knowledge of law in a year at a law office than in twice that time in school. I could get him a good place tomorrow."

Wendell flushed hotly at the words "our little boy." His father had said that several times lately; was he trying to belittle his son?

"Thank you, Father," Wendell said quickly, before his mother could reply. "I know you have good friends, but I must manage my own way. I hope you do not too much mind my living at home. I haven't any money —"

"Wendell! What a thing to say!" Mrs. Holmes was distressed at the way the talk had turned. "Come in and sit down, both of you. We *want* you to live at home! For pity's sake don't make a duty of it! When you were away, at war, I used to dream that maybe, if you lived to come home, you might stay with us awhile, a long time . . ."

She turned the talk to new bookshelves for his room, to friends he might like to have for supper soon. Tensions eased. The crisis passed. Soon Dr. Holmes was talking of other matters, and Wendell slipped away.

Law Students

Law Student

10

Wendell Holmes' starry-eyed view of the law was badly jolted by the end of his first week as a student. The subjects of lectures sounded fascinating. How did the three elderly lecturers manage to be so dull? Listening was as wearisome as Dr. Holmes had predicted — but Wendell was not ready to admit that to his father. He did walk over to see Uncle John Holmes.

After the death of Grandmother Holmes, the big old house had been sold, and John had taken a small place on Appian Way, nearby. John was at home when Wendell dropped in that Friday afternoon.

"You're a lawyer, Uncle John," Wendell began as he stepped inside the door. "How did you keep your first thrill when you studied law?"

Uncle John stared at Wendell; then he roared with laughter.

"You need food, Wendell," he said, a moment later. "I've got bread and cold corned beef. Let's eat." He led the way to his tiny kitchen, where a housekeeper cooked on certain days; on other days John Holmes looked after himself. Now they made man-sized sandwiches, ate cookies and apples, and Wendell did feel cheered.

"All the same, Uncle John . . ."

"You cannot expect a college to supply thrills," John interrupted. "Read the catalog. Did it promise excitement? No. Those 'elderly professors' you mention are brilliant men — a lawyer, a judge, a jurist. They give you facts. You will have to hunt your own thrills in yourself or in the books you read outside the lectures. Courses simply give direction to your reading and thinking. You'll never make a lawyer if you can't last out a week of dull stuff. I'll wager you don't understand all the words those men use."

"Sometimes I think they must be talking a foreign language," Wendell admitted, subdued by his uncle's tirade. "Equity. Common law. Trespass. Negotiate. I thought I knew those words, but in the lecture meanings seem different."

"Of course. Words have different meanings in every profession. Get out your dictionary. Look along the definitions till you come to the words 'In law.' Read that meaning and remember it. You must know words to listen intelligently."

"You talk like Mr. Emerson," Wendell suddenly remembered. "He told me I'd have to take over myself; to read and think. That's what you mean, isn't it, Uncle John?"

"Exactly. And talk with young lawyer friends. John Ropes will help you. You like John Gray, too. Have an evening with them now and then. They'll help you get on the right trail."

Wendell acted on this advice. His mother invited the two young men to supper. Of course Dr. Holmes led talk there, but he was interesting. Afterward Wendell took his friends up to his study, and they talked till midnight.

On this first evening, and others following, they asked each other many questions.

"What is law?" Wendell wanted to know. "Is it restraints by means of which men in power try to control other men?"

"I'd say that law is rules that have grown out of long experience," Gray suggested.

"Do laws change men?" Ropes asked. "Or do men change laws?"

Such questions could not be answered quickly. Wendell searched in books for answers. He thought he learned more in these evenings than in school. But he admitted that lectures gave him new ideas to discuss. Sometimes other friends joined the lawyers; William James and Henry Bowditch were medical students. Charles Peirce was making mathematics and logic his life work. On such evenings talk ranged over the whole universe; they called it "the Cosmos" in an intimate way that amused and challenged them.

The young men went to campaign meetings now and then, especially if George Shattuck was the speaker. Shattuck was handsome, dark haired, a fine speaker. Wendell enjoyed him and his arguments for voting for Abraham Lincoln.

On election day, Wendell Holmes along with a majority of his fellow citizens voted for Lincoln. War still raged, but the end did seem nearer.

Before Christmas Mr. Robert Morse, a well known Boston lawyer, called at the house on Charles Street.

"I've come to see your son Wendell," he said to Dr. Holmes. "I hope I catch him at home?" Wendell was called.

"Good afternoon, Holmes," Mr. Morse said. "I won't keep you long. I need help in my office. How would you like to work there — afternoons when you haven't a lecture?"

Dr. Holmes opened his lips to say "Yes." Then he caught his wife's eye and swallowed the word. Morse went on.

"There's no pay. But you will see how law school theories apply in practice. Like the idea?"

"I like it very much, sir," Wendell said. "And I thank you for asking me." Dr. Holmes relaxed. Wendell had *some* sense.

"May I start tomorrow?"

"Just what I hoped you would say," Morse replied. Talk turned to weather — which was bad — and Morse left.

Wendell had no doubt as to how this opportunity had come to him. But by this time, he had learned that his father was right on one point: experience as well as theory was valuable. He welcomed a job in a good office.

Daily Wendell Holmes went back and forth between Cambridge and Boston. The winter seemed the coldest in memory. Way into March, feet stiffened with cold in spite of piles of straw on streetcar floors.

In Washington, Lincoln's second Inaugural Day was bleak and windy. But crowds gathered, expecting wise suggestions for ending the war. Many were disappointed. This second address was thoughtful and religious rather than political or practical. It sounded like a gentle preparation for peace without harshness.

At Dane Hall students gathered to talk.

"Lincoln's fine words are well enough, but I wish he had spelled out his position," a second year student said. "How is all this going to be done?"

"And the war not yet over," grunted another.

"It will be soon," Wendell Holmes felt sure. "Likely Lincoln has plans he can't tell till then."

Richmond fell on the second day of April. Lee surrendered on the ninth. When this news came, Boston stopped work to celebrate. Crowds thronged the Common, jubilantly retelling the good news. Women with long black mourning veils met women whose men would return and tears of mourning and thankfulness mingled. Mrs. Holmes watched her tall son, alive by a miracle — by three miracles.

"The Union's saved! Now Lincoln can do something!" This idea in various words was repeated over and over.

Someone began to sing "The Union forever, Hurrah, boys, Hurrah!" The crowd took it up and sang happily. Youths joined together, hands on shoulders and snaked through the massed people, singing and whistling loudly. It was a wonderful day. The nation's troubles were over.

One week later Abraham Lincoln was dead. Flags dropped to half mast. Black crepe streamed from windows as a stunned nation mourned.

Incredibly, Andrew Johnson took the oath of office — who had ever thought that *Johnson* would be president? But in time, national and personal business was resumed as usual.

Work filled Wendell Holmes' days and evenings. Mornings he heard two or three lectures and worked in the law library. Afternoons he sat on a stool before a high wall desk in Mr. Morse's office and copied documents. Often he did errands; to the courthouse, another lawyer's office, to the library. Lawyers called this "leg work," a true name.

In spite of chores, Wendell liked work in the office. Mr. Morse had a large and varied business. Wendell learned to have respect for the man's quick decisions; for his careful preparation of a case.

Evenings, Wendell studied a while after supper. Then friends dropped in, or he went out to see them. Dr. Holmes always noticed when Wendell took his hat from the rack.

"Where are you going, Wendell?" he'd call.

Wendell told him, politely. But he came to hate the ever watchful eye that sent him back to childhood. He seemed to have less independence than Amelia. She was a young lady, now, a member of one of the elite Boston Sewing Circles. She came and went as she pleased. Wendell, still a student, seemed a boy to his father.

"Who lectured this morning?" he would ask.

"What books did you take from the library today?"

"Anything new in Morse's office?"

When she was near, Mrs. Holmes came to her son's rescue and changed the subject. One evening she drew Wendell into the dining room after supper and talked to him anxiously.

"Your father is interested in you, Wendell. You mustn't

mind his curiosity. He is proud of everything you are doing."

"I know, Mother," Wendell said with good humor. "It's just Father's way."

But it was a "way" that fretted Wendell. He considered leaving law school and earning some money — but that was silly when his tuition and living made no hardship for his parents. He should be patient and finish his education.

By late spring the long hours of work began to show on Wendell's health. His father fussed about his loss of weight, his paleness. Dr. Holmes rented a house on Nahant — a long strip of sandy beach thrust out into the bay — and he insisted that Wendell stop all work for a while.

Nahant was a popular place with friends of the Holmes family. Their house was invaded by young men eager to enjoy Amelia's company; Wendell saw his little sister with her following. She was "little," but very much the ruler of her world.

"I can't believe this grown-up young lady is the fat little girl I used to drag to parades," Wendell remarked to his mother.

"*I* can't believe you are the same little boy," she teased him. "Your father can't understand how you got to be so tall when both your parents are small. Have you passed six foot three yet, Wendie?" Wendell grinned. He wasn't going to get into that conversation.

The Dixwells had a summer house at Nahant, too, and Wendell dropped in there often. He never planned ahead; just took it for granted that when he came Fanny would want to see him. And she always did.

At the summer's end the same full program of work began — school, office, study and talk. In the back of his mind all this time Wendell felt the need for a special book about law. He did not find it. He spoke to Uncle John about it.

"I want to find out how *law* came to be," he said. "I don't mean laws passed by Parliament, Congress, or legislatures. I mean *law;* law for all people, beginning ages ago, I should think. Did law have a small beginning and grow by logic? Or by man's experience? Is the foundation of law the same anywhere?"

Uncle John puffed at his pipe thoughtfully.

"I don't think I ever heard of such a book," he finally decided. "No. I doubt if there is one. Likely you'll have to write it yourself, Wendell." They had a good laugh at that silly idea.

Wendell dropped in around the corner to tell Fanny about the book he could not find. Not that Fanny knew anything about law; a girl wouldn't, of course. But she listened well. Wendell even repeated Uncle John's remark — that Wendell should write the book himself. She didn't laugh.

"Of course you will, Wendell," she said, amazing him.

Wendell Holmes received his degree in law late in the winter of 1866. He was through with lectures. The degree did not allow him to practice law in the courts, but it was a big step in that direction.

His parents astonished him with a surprise they had planned. He was to go to Europe before he settled down to further study. He could hardly believe his good fortune.

"Now I can talk again with Leslie Stephen," Wendell said. He had enjoyed that young Englishman who had visited in Boston. "And maybe I can see men whose books I have read. You are very kind and generous to me. I do thank you."

Dr. Holmes wrote a couple of letters which might pave the way for such meetings as his son wanted. The doctor had recently been abroad himself, to meet many readers of his books and to receive honors and a degree. Wendell's trip promised many pleasures and added education.

Shortly before Wendell was to sail, Mr. Shattuck sent a

message; would Wendell Holmes kindly call at the office?

"I've been watching you, young man," Shattuck said as he greeted Wendell. "You'll want to study for your bar examinations when you come back, won't you?"

"Yes, sir. That is my plan."

"I suggest that you do your reading in my office. We'll have a corner for you. Someone can stop to answer a question — you'll have many."

"Oh, thank you, sir!" Wendell flushed with pleasure. "I can't imagine anything that would please me more."

On his way home he marveled again at his good fortune — a trip and the added joy of a definite task on his return.

He sailed away in high spirits.

Fanny Dixwell, looking lovely in spite of being thin and pale, spent the summer at the beach, being determinedly gay. She fooled most people — but not Mrs. Holmes, Edward, or Uncle John.

A Lawyer's Oath

11

Suffolk County Court House

Wendell Holmes liked London. His letter to Leslie Stephen brought that one-time Boston visitor calling at once. The next day he came again with his brother Fitzjames, the judge; with true friendliness they planned sightseeing and parties so that the visitor could meet interesting people.

As he went about, Holmes saw that Leslie Stephen's reputation as a philosopher and critic had grown; he was highly esteemed. He found, too, that people liked his father's books. They talked of the "Breakfast Table" essays, now grown to several volumes, and of the novel *Elsie Venner*. Soon they liked Wendell for himself.

"An attractive young man; modest, too," was said of him.

Holmes saw famous sights, visited museums and galleries, and did a daily round of parties.

"When you first came," Leslie Stephen recalled one day, "you said there was one man you must see — who is he?"

"John Stuart Mill," Holmes replied. "His work fascinates

me. Am I being too bold to want to meet him?"

"Indeed, no," Stephen assured him. "But Mill lives out of London. I'll write and plan the call at his convenience."

As he awaited the interview, Holmes thought over various books of Mill's that he had read. John Stuart Mill was a philosopher and economist; he was interested in wages and hours of labor and other practical matters. The man must have a rare mind, Holmes thought. It was said that he read and understood Plato before he was ten years old. Knowing something of Plato himself, Wendell was eager to meet a man who turned philosophy to problems of business.

The day came. The great man was cordial to his young visitor and talked freely. Mill was older than Mr. Emerson; he fidgeted, was bald and nervous.

"I tell you as I told Parliament," he said, "we must think of the greatest good for the greatest number. For this I am called a radical. Some day they will see that I am right."

Holmes listened avidly to new thoughts about labor. He tried to remember each sentence so that he could mull it over later.

In a few days the Stephen brothers and Holmes crossed the channel for sightseeing on the continent. They ended the tour with a stay in Switzerland. The rugged Alps were a revelation of beauty to the New Englander. The snowy heights, the fertile valleys, the industrious people, charmed him.

The three young men joined a group of mountain climbers, and since Holmes enjoyed the climb so much, they went again on a more difficult expedition. This was the first sport

that Wendell Holmes had ever really enjoyed. He liked to be roped in line; it was a challenge to clutch at an icy ledge with numb fingers as his toes in clumsy shoes groped for foothold. He felt a kind of exaltation in these great efforts.

"Is it the philosopher in you?" Leslie asked, half teasing.

"Maybe." Holmes had no breath for talk. As he paused, looking around at the vast panorama, a new thought came to him. Our struggle upward here is like life; tied to fellowmen, searching a safe place to stand, ever reaching higher.

"This is like life," Leslie said, as though he shared Wendell's unspoken thought, "struggle, and success at the summit. Every person needs the thrill of success — we will experience it in another hour."

Wendell Holmes left Switzerland reluctantly.

At home, in September, no one seemed excited about either John Stuart Mill or Switzerland. For a few hours Amelia listened, prodding Wendell to talk about London parties and fashions. Dr. Holmes was pleased to hear that his English readers wanted a sequel to *Elsie Venner*. Edward, now an important senior at Harvard, was in Cambridge. Wendell felt quite left on his own.

Uncle John will listen, he thought, and set off for Cambridge. John Holmes' first words surprised his nephew.

"Get a file of back newspapers, Wendell, and catch up on doings in Boston. There's been a printers' strike. Talk about an eight-hour day stirs the city. Employers can't see what a workman will do with his spare time if he works only eight hours, six days a week."

This caught Wendell's attention.

"What do workmen say?" he asked.

"You'd be surprised. Some say a man can do more and better work in eight than in ten hours. One bold fellow says that a workman's time, after work, is his own. Amazing! Why, it's not long since mill owners said women had to work twelve hours a day to keep them out of mischief. I tell you, Nephew, the world is changing. Seen Fanny yet?"

"Well, not yet." The shift of topic surprised Wendell.

"I do not understand you, Wendell," Uncle John exclaimed. "Coming here to talk to án old man when a pretty girl awaits nearby. Get along with you, or I'll disown you!"

After he got to the Dixwells, Wendell regretted that he had not come the first day he was at home. Fanny was so pretty, so interested in his talk. He told her about Mill and Switzerland. Mrs. Dixwell invited him to stay to supper; he had a wonderful time.

On Monday morning, Wendell Holmes went to the office of Chandler, Shattuck, and Thayer to start his studies for the bar examination. On passing this he would be allowed to practice law. Young lawyer friends had assured him that the examinations were easy.

"Just memorize everything that has been asked before."

"If you'd had the sense to read in Shattuck's office instead of going to law school you might have got by without an examination," another said.

Wendell doubted this. He would not even have liked "getting by." He needed all he had learned at law school. Now, this morning he met the three partners and was assigned to a desk.

"I have a list of books for you, Mr. Holmes," Thayer said. "Coke on Littleton, Montesquieu on the spirit of the law, Mill on logic, Stephen on criminal law."

"It will be fine to reread Mill and Stephen since I have met them," Holmes said and settled to work.

Holmes liked the feeling in the office. He liked Mr. Thayer, and he very much liked being called "Mr. Holmes."

Autumn passed, and the holidays. February had nearly ended before Mr. Shattuck decided that Holmes was ready for the bar examination. He wrote the letter of character recommendation required and made arrangements.

Holmes wondered if he would be frightened. The ordeal was not a written examination; it was oral. The examining lawyers were to ask him anything they chose.

But when he faced his questioners around a table, he was not frightened. His mind was clear, his thoughts quick. They did ask some tricky questions; but he had the answers. After a couple of hours the thing was done.

"You pass with flying colors," one said, smiling.

"But it was so easy." Holmes protested, surprised.

"Few find it easy. You were well prepared. That makes all the difference in the world. I predict a fine future for you in law, Mr. Holmes."

Wendell could hardly wait to get outside where he could show his delight and relief. He wanted to run around the Common, to shout his glee. Instead he went back to the office — but he got generous congratulations there.

"Our senior partner will go with you Monday when you take the lawyer's oath," Mr. Shattuck said, pleased with Holmes.

Monday, March 4, 1867, was a bleak day. A chill wind blew as Mr. Chandler and Wendell Holmes walked to the Suffolk County Court House. This was the building where Anthony Burns had been jailed almost thirteen years before. Holmes had gone in and out hundreds of times in his years of studying law. But as he walked between the marble pillars this day the old building seemed to take on a new dignity.

They entered the Superior Court room of the County of Suffolk of the Commonwealth of Massachusetts. They sat in the lawyers' seats, at right angles to the bench behind which was the great chair for the judge.

Holmes glanced around. Only a few sat in the seats for the public, this early Monday morning. Dr. Holmes was among these in the second row. He had not spoken of coming; Wendell was pleased to see him.

Judge Lord entered, his curly hair well brushed. His long black robe fluttered as he took his place.

The clerk stepped forward.

"Hear ye! Hear ye!" he called in the traditional way. "The Court will now attend to the taking of the oath."

This was Holmes' cue. He stepped forward and took his place before the bench. All the people stood up.

Judge Lord stood, holding a Bible in his hand. He looked solemn, but friendly, too, as Holmes laid his right hand on the sacred book and repeated from memory the words of his pledge:

"I solemnly swear that I will do no falsehood or consent to the doing of any in Court; I will not wittingly or willingly promote or sue any false, groundless or unlawful suit, nor give aid nor consent to the same; I will delay no man for lucre or malice; but I will conduct myself in the office of an attorney within the Court according to the best of my knowledge and discretion, and with all good fidelity as well to the Courts as my clients. So help me God."

Judge Lord bowed. The clerk stepped forward and motioned Holmes to sign the register. The ceremony was over.

"March 4. Oliver Wendell Holmes, Junior," the new attorney wrote. The final word ended in a flourish.

Mr. Shattuck had invited several friends to drop in at the office. There was much congratulating and handshaking.

When he got away, Wendell stopped at a printer's shop and left an order. A couple of days later he opened the small parcel the printer's boy delivered and studied the new cards:

OLIVER WENDELL HOLMES, JR.
COUNSELLOR AT LAW

On a sudden impulse, he enclosed one in an envelope and

sent it to the secretary of the Class of 1861, Harvard. Now I shall be something besides a poet, he thought.

The next few days seemed blank, dull. He had worked so hard toward that examination that he felt aimless, now, by contrast. Books were still there to be read — but where should he begin?

At home, Edward was hunting through back newspapers to collect articles about the suggested impeachment of President Johnson.

"Why are you interested, Neddy?" Wendell asked. "It's a political matter." Wendell had little interest in politics.

"There's a legal aspect we're supposed to study," Edward said, laughing. "Maybe you're not interested in law?"

Thus prodded, Wendell did study the matter. It helped fill empty days.

While he had been studying for the examination, Wendell had neglected his friends. Now he found they were scattered or too busy for visiting. Will James was in Europe in the hope of improving his health. Wendell missed Will. Their minds stimulated each other. They even liked the same girl.

"I hear Will James went to Europe to keep from falling in love with Fanny Dixwell," Amelia said pertly, at supper. "That gives you a clear field, Wendie. Fanny liked Will, but he thought you had first chance."

"*Mother!*" Wendell was shocked. "How can you let Amelia gossip like that?"

"Is it gossip, Son? For all I know it may be true."

Months dragged by. November had come when he got his

first case. His client wished to sue the New York Central Railroad for the accidental death of her husband.

"I'll help you in court," Mr. Shattuck promised. "But you must do all the work of preparation."

Wendell went at that case as though his life depended on winning it. He had every fact verified and ready. Mr. Shattuck was brilliant as usual in court. But they lost the case. Holmes was actually numb with surprise. He had worked so hard; had believed so firmly that their case was just — what sort of law could decide against them?

Late in that miserable day he went to see Uncle John.

"So you lost," John said, glancing at his nephew. "Well, that's law for you, but you would have it. Come with me to the Dixwells. I promised to come over."

Wendell dragged along, feeling blue.

"You lost?" Fanny exclaimed as she saw Wendell. "Well, cases have been lost before. Don't take it so hard."

"But Shattuck was wonderful! I had all the facts . . ." Wendell was still dazed with that verdict. The evening was not a success.

More months went by. Edward was in law school and doing well. He was a handsome youth; not as tall as his brother, and thin. He had asthma like his Uncle John. Edward had a cordial manner; Wendell seemed a plodder by contrast.

Both his sons were still dependent, but Dr. Holmes did not mind. He prospered as did many other Americans at this time. He lectured, wrote books and essays, saved money and bought stock in companies that were developing America.

General Grant was elected president in the fall of 1868, and the country rolled along easily.

Dr. Holmes, with other Bostonians, had been watching changes in his city. Land had been made by filling in along the Back Bay, making a whole new section, much of it desirable for homes. He bought a lot and built a new house — number 296 Beacon Street. It was one of a row of narrow four-story brick houses, high, in the fashion of the day. His sons had rooms on the third floor.

Lawyer Holmes had little interest in the new house except to be glad his mother was so pleased. He was in the depths of discouragement. Three facts taunted him; he was a dependent in his father's house, he hardly earned his spending money. And he would soon be thirty years old.

While a soldier, Wendell Holmes had often been cold and wet, ill-fed and hungry, but his dreams had sustained him. Now comforts surrounded him, but where were the dreams? Had he aimed too high for his capacities? Was he marked for failure? These questions haunted him, and he found no answers.

296 Beacon Street

Getting His Stride

A message rescued Wendell Holmes just when he had reached the end of his patience, waiting for clients. Mr. Thayer would like to see him about some editing. Holmes went at once to Thayer's office.

"A new edition of Kent's *Commentaries* is to be published," Mr. Thayer began, "and I am to be the editor. I would like to have you assist me."

Holmes' eyes sparkled, and new life seemed to flow into him. This would be work of importance. James Kent of New York was a great judge and jurist; many lawyers considered him the founder of American law. His four-volume work, *Commentaries on American Law*, published in the late 1820's, explained the laws of his country and commented on court decisions. Kent himself had kept his work up to date until his death in 1847; there had been, in all, eleven editions of the *Commentaries*.

"I'll do my best, sir," Holmes said.

"Good. I'm glad you will undertake the job," Mr. Thayer was pleased. "It is no easy task that I am giving you," he added. "You will have to search American and English court records for cases that have a bearing on laws Kent included. The pay is trifling. The work will be tedious — probably take two years."

"Only two years!" Holmes exclaimed.

"Can't give you more time."

"I'll do my best, sir," Holmes promised again. He could hardly wait to start on volume one.

Wendell Holmes liked this new work. It was hard; but it was his own. He searched through masses of court decisions to see what laws were still useful. The nation was constantly changing. A new edition of Kent would show judges which laws were being followed.

Will James returned from Europe and expected long evenings of talk. Holmes was glad to see him. But his interest in the Cosmos was slight compared with his fascination for Kent. Will wrote to his brother Henry that Wendell Holmes was studying "like a person possessed. He seldom goes out even on Saturday nights!"

Another friend wrote that Holmes carried a green bag with him — his precious Kent and notebook inside — on the rare times when he was persuaded to accept an invitation.

"He sets this bag under his chair at the dinner table," this letter continued. "He looks thin and pale."

So much of the work on Kent was thinking, deciding. It had to be done alone. And those two short years made him work every possible minute.

Meanwhile, Edward Holmes graduated with honors from Harvard Law School. There had been no argument as to where he should study. Since Wendell entered that school, it was already gaining in prestige. After Edward was admitted to the bar, Wendell resigned from Chandler, Shattuck, and Thayer and the brothers opened their own office, Holmes and Holmes.

Both were determined to build up a good practice. But there were difficulties. Edward's easy way was attractive, but dreadful asthma threatened his health. Wendell was absorbed by Kent evenings and some days.

"I don't know about this partnership," Dr. Holmes fretted to his wife. "Edward will do his share, but Wendell is so slow, so possessed with study . . ."

"Wendell is the kind that gets a slow start," she said loyally.

"A slow start! Where is he going when he does start?"

No one, not even Wendell, seemed to notice that from the time it was known that he had begun on the *Commentaries*, work came to him. He was invited to review new law books. At first these reviews were unsigned. Then his signature was used, showing that the review had value because it was his opinion. This pleased his father.

The brothers enjoyed being together. They worked hard. But to Wendell, clients were an interruption to the important business of editing Kent.

"Wendell was right, long ago," Mrs. Holmes remarked to Amelia. "He likes study; he wants to be a jurist, not a practicing lawyer. But how is he to earn a living?"

Amelia laughed. Earning a living did not bother her. Dr. Holmes' varied work and dividends continued to bring prosperity. In time business improved for Holmes and Holmes, too. Wendell got his first case and won it. Edward was very happy.

"We're going forward from now, Father," he said at supper. "You will be proud of your sons yet."

Soon Edward's engagement to Henrietta Wigglesworth, of a wealthy Boston family, was announced. Amelia had a steady beau and talked about a wedding. Only the older brother was untouched by romance. Oh, he liked Fanny, but that was no romance, though Amelia teased him unmercifully.

Wendell hardly heard her. His reviews of law books won him a place on the editorial staff of the *American Law Review*. He could not refuse that distinction, even for Kent.

Charles W. Eliot, a tutor, then a professor, had been chosen president of Harvard in 1869. His new ideas made quite a stir in the university's sedate halls. He was promptly called a "radical" because his ideas differed from traditional ways. Eliot organized new courses. He gave credit for work in science and started new methods of teaching.

In a couple of years he got around to the law school. For it, he engaged younger lecturers, among them Wendell Holmes and Wendell's wartime friend, John Gray.

"I want you to show students how law has developed in America," Eliot told Holmes in their interview. "You are working on that as you edit Kent." Holmes was pleased that Eliot had noticed the work with Mr. Thayer.

"I accept with pleasure," Holmes said. "I'll try to make

students see that while English law is our foundation, we adapt it to American life — that's what you want?"

"Exactly!" The men parted, both satisfied.

Later in the day Wendell told Edward about the talk.

"If lecturing didn't fit with Kent, I suppose you would have refused the Harvard appointment," Edward said. His voice had a trace of bitterness.

"Of course! Kent is important."

Edward sniffed. Perhaps it was just his asthma.

Soon Edward and then Amelia married, the weddings not many weeks apart. In the big house at 296 Beacon Street, dinners and suppers were gay as ever; Dr. Holmes always had guests. But Wendell missed his sister and brother at breakfasts.

"What are you teaching today, Wendie?"

"Are your classes larger?"

"What do the students think of Eliot's frills?"

The doctor hardly waited for answers. He had no confidence in Wendell's observation of such matters.

With his sister and brother gone, Wendell began to feel another loss. He missed Fanny Dixwell. For years, except when at war or in Europe, Wendell Holmes had seen Fanny every week — often several times each week. While at college and law school, he often dropped by to see her. After he began work on Kent, he stopped going to Cambridge except to rush out to give a lecture.

But he often saw Fanny in his own home, having tea with Amelia; he came to count on it. After Amelia was married,

Fanny went to her new home, not to 296 Beacon Street.

"Have you had a quarrel with Fanny?" he asked his mother one day. "She hasn't been here all week."

"All week!" his mother was amazed. "She hasn't been here since Christmas. Why should she come? Amelia no longer lives here. Have *you* quarreled with Fanny, Wendell?"

"Of course not! She should come to see you. Why not ask her to tea, Mother?"

"Well, I could." Mrs. Holmes' tone was doubtful. She wondered whether it had always been too easy for Wendell to be with Fanny. "But you know, Son, streetcars run both ways between Boston and Cambridge."

"Oh, streetcars! Ask Uncle John to drive her over. I'd like to see him, too."

When they came to tea a few days later Mrs. Holmes was shocked at Fanny's appearance. Thin, pale — she looked defeated, quite unlike the glowing Fanny.

Mrs. Holmes drew her toward the fire in the parlor; the March day was chilly. John Holmes lingered, hanging up his coat and muffler as Wendell came down the stairs. He had not been feeling well of late.

"What's the matter with you, Uncle John?" Wendell exclaimed.

"I have a dumb nephew who worries me," John Holmes said in a brusque tone. "The fellow can't see beyond a printed page. Likes a book better than a pretty girl who's loved him for years. If there's one thing above another makes me sick, it's a dumb man named Holmes."

"*Uncle John!*" Wendell stared at this tirade.

"See for yourself — if you've not forgotten how," John said and stepped into the parlor, shutting off talk.

Wendell followed. His face and neck were scarlet, his manner shaken and confused. His mother served the tea and cakes, and the three chatted. Wendell sat silent, eyeing Fanny. Yes, she *was* thin. She looked weary.

Fanny saw his covert glances; she was oppressed by his silence. Finally she could stand it no longer.

"I really must be going," she said.

"Oh, not yet!" John Holmes exclaimed. "I haven't finished the cakes." Fanny had only crumpled hers.

"Uncle John!" Wendell stood up, nearly shattering his

teacup. "You stay here with Mother. If Fanny has to go, I'll drive her home and come back for you."

Fanny looked up in surprise. She did not object.

In a masterful, direct way his mother had not seen for a long time, Wendell got Fanny's wraps and his own and they went off. Uncle John stayed for supper. He stayed on, and on. And still Wendell — and the borrowed horse and buggy — did not return.

Mrs. Holmes was about to suggest that John had better stay for the night when Wendell arrived.

"Fanny and I are going to be married," he announced without preamble. "Do you mind if we live here a while, Father? You know how little my lecturing pays, and writing, and the few cases we have. Do you *mind*, Father?"

Anxious eyes studied his father's face. Lack of income affected Wendell deeply. It made no difference that his father had plenty. He wanted to pay his own way.

"Mind?" the little doctor got up and slapped his tall son's shoulders. "I'd like a daughter in the house again. It's about time you got around to this step. Do you realize that you are thirty-one?"

"I didn't notice, Father. I guess I've always meant to marry Fanny, but I forgot to tell her. We . . ."

The three waited, silent.

"If it's all right, we'll be married in June."

"This is wonderful news," Mrs. Holmes said and pulled her son's face down to kiss him. Uncle John grinned. Why hadn't he prodded the boy before? Hated to meddle, likely.

"I'll get at cleaning and fixing up the third floor rooms," Mrs. Holmes planned. "With Neddy gone, you and Fanny can have the whole floor to yourselves. We'll like that, Son."

"I can tell all my old stories," the doctor boasted. "Fanny's not been here for so long, I may have new ones. She'll laugh even if they are old. Wonderful girl." Dr. Holmes continued to be pleased with his world.

Now that plans were made, Wendell was radiantly happy. Why had he waited so long? He didn't know.

On the seventeenth of June, 1872, Fanny Dixwell and Oliver Wendell Holmes, Jr. were married. They did not take a grand tour, as fashionable brides and grooms were doing then.

"Fancy taking a tour with Kent in a green bag!" Fanny confided to a friend. "My Wendell has work to do. That's more important than a tour."

Mrs. Holmes had made the third floor charming in her own way. Now Fanny, without the slightest fuss, deftly made it hers. She loved the entrancing view. She valued the kindness that surrounded her. She did not mind when Dr. Holmes asked his usual question, "Where are you going now, Fanny?" as she came down the stairs. He was just interested; she understood him.

Evenings, Wendell's friends took to dropping in again.

Fanny made them welcome, and the talk was good. Gently, skillfully, she guided it from the Cosmos to law, and Wendell did not miss an evening away from Kent. He wrote better for these changes.

Young Mrs. Holmes was making a good beginning.

13 "The Common Law"

Big Ben—London

The twelfth edition of *Kent's Commentaries* was published in 1873; soon after, cautious but favorable reviews came out in law journals. In London, when the volumes arrived, they were acclaimed.

"The best edition yet published."

"New and original points of view about law."

These and other words of praise were pleasant reading for Mr. Thayer and Wendell Holmes.

When clippings from English journals came to the United States, American reviewers published the flattering phrases they read in the English reviews.

"Will James is furious!" a friend told Wendell. "This just shows that Americans are copycats, he says. Haven't minds of their own!"

"American reviewers will learn to stand on their own feet some day," Holmes said tolerantly. "It's natural that they are slow to praise. English law is our foundation."

Fanny clipped notices and treasured every one. All this would encourage Wendell and add to his reputation. She took the clippings to his parents so they could enjoy the praise.

Lecturing at Harvard went well, too. President Eliot and Dean Langdell of the law school encouraged Holmes to teach in a new way — they called it "the case method." It was the method of the laboratory applied to law.

These three men believed that students would understand and remember better if general facts were illustrated by actual cases. So Holmes hunted out legal cases that showed how a certain law had been applied.

"Do you agree that the judge was right in his decision?" Holmes would ask. "*Why* do you agree?"

"Why do you disagree?" he asked of dissenters.

"Holmes is forever asking 'why,'" a student complained.

"But his class is the most interesting in the school," another said. "He doesn't just talk." More students enrolled in his course the next term.

In the late spring of '73, Mr. Shattuck came to 296 Beacon Street. Fanny, at his request, took him upstairs. He had a purposeful air that excited her.

"I'm breaking away from my old firm, Wendell," he began in his quick way. "Bill Monroe is going with me, and we want you to join us — will you?"

Fanny flushed with joy — this was a big compliment. Then she wondered — would Wendell go into a new law office? Kent was finished. Mr. Shattuck would not ask him to give up lectures; those brought prestige. But to sit in an office . . .

"Thank you!" Wendell was saying in a pleased tone. He knew this invitation was an honor. "But what good will I be to you? I'm no hand to get business — Edward learned that."

He's going to decline and I can't bear it, Fanny thought.

"Oh, business." Shattuck waved the word aside. "Monroe and I aren't bad at that. But we think it will be a good idea to have in the firm a man who knows law as you do, Wendell. We'd count on you to keep us in the straight and narrow . . ."

"Then I accept, and thank you, sir," Wendell decided quickly. Fanny relaxed, her eyes shining.

Holmes had expected that he would be the third member of the new firm; that seemed fair enough. But when he walked into the new office the sign read:

SHATTUCK, HOLMES, AND MONROE

Fanny went over to see it and gloat — privately.

In spite of this good fortune, affairs did not prosper materially for the young couple, because that summer of 1873 the nation was stricken with a terrible depression. People were in a panic. Factories closed, and new ones were not built. Railroads did not expand. Dividends stopped. People who had intended to get legal advice or to start a suit in court waited.

Life at 296 Beacon Street was not much changed; there was money enough for simple pleasures the Holmes family most enjoyed. Dr. Holmes' close supervision of Wendell and Fanny did not change, either.

Wendell is earning, Fanny told herself. It's just that he has so much less than his father. I must find some place for us to live, even one room. Wendell will never notice what it is if I am happy.

For an hour, Fanny sat there, looking out over the river, thinking. Then she wandered around the room — there was little here that was her own. No crib. No need for a nursery. She had so hoped for the baby that did not come.

Suddenly she shook off her mood and put on her hat and coat. "I'll find a place of our own!" She spoke the words aloud, with determination.

The search took weeks, but finally she found two rooms over a drugstore next door to the Boston Athenaeum. Wendell would like that. The rooms had one great advantage; they were cheap. Gaily she took Wendell to see the place.

"But will you like this, Fanny?" he exclaimed. He had not known of her long search.

"Of course! Would I have brought you if I was not sure? I'll put your desk here and the bookcase there. Look at this newfangled thing for cooking — they call it a 'gas-ring.' I'll make breakfast on it. I'll get a good lamp . . ."

Wendell watched her, hardly noticing her words. She looked so pretty in her full skirts and tiny waist, in the fetching bonnet. He liked the glow on her eager face.

"We'll take it," he agreed. He had confidence in Fanny.

Soon they were settled. Fanny was skillful about breakfast; porridge first, then coffee and eggs on the gas-ring. They went out for dinners, holding hands and running down the curving street to Tremont and around the corner to the Parker House. They often found friends eating there, and brought

them back for talk.

One evening, as they started up the hill, the fire bells rang
out and the red fire engine drawn by galloping, straining horses
dashed by.

"Let's follow them!" Fanny cried. They grabbed hands and
ran like children to the fire.

It was a beautiful blaze. The roof of an old building fell
with a mounting shower of sparks lighting the sky.

"I used to go to fires, when I was a boy," Wendell remembered. "Father loved to chase fires. The department puts them
out so soon now."

"Your father told me yesterday that you ought to exercise more," Fanny said, as they strolled home. "I shall tell him how fast you ran tonight. He'll be surprised."

Most evenings lawyer Holmes worked on cases, new cases for the office, old cases to illustrate his lectures. A variation was the reading of new law books on which he wrote reviews. Often he would stop, pen in hand, and try out a sentence on Fanny.

Sitting across the table, Fanny stuck her needle into her embroidery and listened carefully.

"Now tell it back to me," he would say. If she had not quite grasped the idea, he tried again, until she understood. Then he wrote rapidly, getting those sentences down.

One evening he began to write an article on liability, debt. Ideas about liability were in men's earliest laws. Holmes wondered how far man's responsibility should hold in the changing world. The responsibility of a "common carrier" was relatively simple when men rode in stagecoaches or carts. What was a just law when railroads made a vast network across the land and thousands of ships carried passengers? Did old laws deal fairly with owners, workers, and passengers? Holmes' ideas on this got a wide reading.

By thrift and good fortune, Fanny and Wendell managed a modest trip to London. It was to be an advantage for Holmes to confer with his friends, the Stephen brothers and Charles Peirce and Frederick Pollock. Fanny looked forward to the journey.

Wendell was feted and made much of in London. He visited the English courts. He talked late on various current cases. He was asked to write for English law journals.

These honors delighted Fanny. But ere long the formal
dinners grew tedious. She began exploring London alone. She
haunted old markets, delighting in curious things. One day she
happened upon a dainty glass perfume bottle, the price so small
that she could buy it.

When Wendell came to dress for a dinner, she regaled him
with a tale of the market and the odd little man who had sold
her the beautiful bottle.

"You know, Wendell, I'm going to collect perfume bottles."

"Such an idea," he leaned back, laughing. Fanny always
was entertaining. It was not until he was dressed that he
noticed she had not changed.

"We haven't much time," he said kindly.

"Oh, you go and give my regrets," Fanny said. "I hate
to rush." After this he often went without her. And Fanny collected six charming perfume bottles, each with a tale.

America, Boston, looked wonderful to her when they got
home. "I love it here," she told Dr. Holmes. "Wendell loves
London — but give me Boston, always."

As the 1870's passed, the nation recovered from the depression. Grant's eight years in the White House ended without much honor to himself. Brilliant as a general, as a chief
executive he had left too much to underlings. Many of these
men were selfish and disloyal.

Rutherford B. Hayes was elected the next president by such
a narrow margin that the result was not known until late in
February. Hayes had been a general in the Civil War, too; he

surprised the nation by taking hold of his country's affairs with loyalty and vigor.

In the autumn Wendell Holmes was invited to give a series of lectures on law at the Lowell Institute. In 1836 a Mr. John Lowell had organized a group of people who wanted more education even though they had passed school age. Three years later the Institute was opened to the public. By 1880 several series of lectures were offered each season. Dr. Holmes had given a series on literature one year. Likely the growing popularity of Wendell Holmes' lectures at Harvard helped bring him this opportunity. He was to give twelve lectures.

"You accepted?" Fanny asked.

"Indeed I did." Wendell smiled at her eagerness. "This is exactly the chance I want. I'll take my law school lectures, my articles and book reviews, and tie them all together. I'll show how law changes. How legislators make laws and judges apply them to fit the needs of the people. Do you see what I mean, Fanny?"

Fanny nodded. What she saw was that Wendell was happy. Of course more evenings would be spent by the lamp in their tiny sitting room. She'd better get a new piece of embroidery tomorrow and some more silks. She would need them.

As his work developed the idea came to Wendell Holmes that these lectures might be made into a book.

"Do you remember that once I hunted a book which would tell these very facts I now plan to use? I couldn't find it. Uncle John said I should write it — and we laughed."

"I didn't laugh." Fanny could remember, too. "I thought
you might do it. I still think that, Wendell."

Pleased, Holmes ruffled through his notes. "I have planned
for twelve lectures, the last a summary of the eleven. Listeners
need a summary. Readers do not. I shall have plenty of material for a book. What do you think, Fanny?"

"It's a wonderful idea, Wendell. As a book, your work will
seem more permanent — not just words, gone on the air. You
must do it."

"Time runs out," he said presently, surprising her. "A man

should do something in his chosen field by the time he is forty — 1881 will soon be here and there is much to do. How is this paragraph, Fanny . . ."

The lectures were acclaimed, the attendance was flattering. Wendell Holmes looked dignified and handsome. He had grown a mustache, in the fashion of the day; it was supposed to break the line of his long thin face. His eager absorption in his subject held listeners. No one noticed his neck.

Fanny saved the excellent reviews each week, but Holmes was too busy to read them; he was ever working on the next lecture.

By the time the course ended, he was getting his material in shape for the book. Then he wrote a preface in which he explained his purpose. He had wanted such a book when he was a student, he wrote. Probably he might never have written it but for the Lowell Lectures; he was grateful for that opportunity.

The title he chose was *The Common Law* — law, he meant, that is basic for all men, common to everyone. In the first chapter he wrote:

"The object of this book is to present a general view of the common law . . . The life of law has not been logic; it has been experience." He explained that the needs of the times, current moral ideals, and public policy, the understanding of the judges — all these help to make the rules by which men are governed. The tale of a nation's growth is told by the development of its laws and that growth is sounder when citizens understand their laws.

"The spirit of law (he wrote) is the feeling of the people at the time. The method of law has come down through history. It is not enough that a law must be familiar, it must fit the needs of the day . . ." These were bold thoughts. Would the public accept them?

He finished the work soon after New Year's Day, 1881. The book was published before March 8th when Holmes was forty.

He brought a copy home and handed it to Fanny with that appealing mixture of pride and modesty which was his.

"You don't have to read it, Fanny," he said. "But here it is. A book."

"Read it!" exclaimed Fanny as she grasped it lovingly. "Wendell! Don't you know that I could say it by heart? The object of this book is to . . ." she glanced up at him roguishly. "Didn't you know that I really *listened* when you read to me?"

Holmes chuckled, and drew her to him.

"Fanny! Of course! And now let's go out and celebrate!"

Harvard Lecture

14

A
Hard
Decision

Publication of *The Common Law* made a difference in Wendell Holmes' life. Reviews in the United States and in England praised it highly. Boston lawyers called at the office to congratulate him, and personal friends crowded the small rooms over the drugstore. Fanny was radiant.

From a distance men wrote words of praise: "This is a notable work!"

"You have put a solid foundation under American law."

"Your book will have a long life. No law school can be without it."

Such opinions pleased the author. The firm's business increased, reflecting his growing reputation. But Wendell and Fanny Holmes lived on over the drugstore with the same economy and simplicity.

Dr. Holmes enjoyed the praise.

"My little boy does right well," he said, pretending modesty. "I admit it." Fanny laughed when the quip was repeated to her. The doctor was proud as a peacock. She understood that.

At the office Holmes was surrounded by respect and good will. One day as a new client left, Mr. Shattuck remarked, "You'll get a judgeship out of that book, Wendell. When the next vacancy comes up, see if I'm not right."

Wendell smiled. Of course Mr. Shattuck was just being friendly, but the thought lingered in his mind. Did he *want* to be a judge? Or did he prefer teaching? He liked teaching; he did not need to decide now.

Not long after this conversation President Eliot invited Holmes to be a full professor at Harvard Law School. This would give him much more prestige than he had as a lecturer.

"I shall have a contract prepared," Eliot said. "I need not tell you how very happy I am."

But when Holmes told Mr. Shattuck of this honor his partner amazed him by holding back.

"Before you accept, Wendell, be sure you want a life of teaching. I've had a feeling that you are coming to a fork in your road — be sure you take the right turning, *now.*" He paused. "Judge Lord is ill. I hear he is about to resign. That will leave a vacancy in the Supreme Judicial Court of the state. Rumor says that the governor may appoint you in his place. Better have a clause in your contract releasing you if a judgeship is offered."

"Eliot wouldn't like that," Holmes said quickly.

"Of course not. But he won't make an issue of it. He will think that, once he has you, you'll be there always."

Shattuck went into his own office.

The phrase "be there always" startled Holmes and raised the old question: teacher, judge? Which did he want?

Holmes had often spoken of the importance of teaching law. "I have no interest in turning out 'smart lawyers,'" he had said. "I aim to educate wise ones; men who know the meaning of law and have the temperament to practice it." He had enjoyed lecturing. Students trusted Professor Holmes; his classes grew steadily.

But to be a judge . . . to meet all kinds of people, to study many sorts of cases and decide issues. Surely that would be stimulating. This court that Shattuck mentioned was the highest court in his state; it would be an honor and a responsibility to sit on that bench.

Holmes signed the amended contract, and no need for decision arose. But the question about his own future seemed to make him more keenly aware of changes going on in his country.

In that year 1882, a new phrase, "giants of industry," was in headlines. Andrew Carnegie in steel, J. Pierpont Morgan in banking, John D. Rockefeller in oil, James J. Hill in railroads, and a few others had been developing their special fields so fast that law could hardly keep up with them. Labor unions with problems of strikes and picketing were in the public eye, too. Did the nation need better interpretation of old laws, or new laws? Judges by their decisions could help decide that point.

College opened, and Professor Holmes began his work. An unexpected pleasure turned up — the arrival of a young lawyer from Kentucky to lecture at the Law School. This man, Louis Brandeis, was Bohemian-born and only twenty-six. He was tall, thin, intelligent, and energetic. He and Wendell Holmes became friends at once.

In December Professor Holmes was just finishing a morning lecture when he was astonished to have the door open and George Shattuck enter the classroom. Holmes waved the students out; they crowded by the visitor, absorbed in their own talk. Shattuck stepped to the desk.

"Wendell!" His voice had an imperative ring. "Judge Lord has resigned. The governor wants to appoint you. Will you take the judgeship? He wants to know, at the State House. In an hour."

"An hour!" Holmes was dazed. "But . . ."

"No buts about it! Come with me at once!"

"I'd have to resign from the firm *and* the law school." Holmes spoke quietly; he had not moved.

"Of course. A judge cannot practice law and teach. I am thinking of you and work you should do. Eliot will think of Harvard. You must come with me. Get your coat."

Suddenly Wendell Holmes' problem was answered. The need to choose showed him that he wanted to be a judge.

President Eliot did *not* like this resignation, and Holmes could not blame him. The interview was soon over; Shattuck and Holmes caught a Boston streetcar and arrived at the governor's office before his conference began.

A week later the governor made the official announcement of the appointment of Oliver Wendell Holmes, Jr. as judge on the Supreme Court of the Commonwealth of Massachusetts.

Early in January Judge Holmes took the oath of office and his place in the court. Not quite forty-two, he was much the youngest of the seven judges. They were cautious in their welcome. Holmes was young — he would outgrow that. But he was said to be versed in the history and theory of law. He might become troublesome, who knew? Many of the cases were about business matters. Did the new judge know anything about business? Time would have to answer that question.

Every morning, now, Judge Holmes, dressed as custom required in morning coat and striped trousers, left his home for the State House.

One morning his mother chanced to be at their rooms.

"I wish he was to change to a robe," she remarked to Fanny. "Formal suits are well enough, but on the bench judges should be set apart."

"You've always believed in Wendell, haven't you, Mother?" Fanny said. They thought he looked very handsome: his heavy hair touched with gray, his manner direct and energetic; his bearing erect, like a soldier. Behind the curtain they watched with pride as he strode down the street.

In a few days a large dinner was given in honor of the new judge. The mayor was there, with Dr. Holmes beside him. The doctor had been asked to write a poem in honor of the occasion; he enjoyed such a task. When he rose to read it an ovation greeted him. Men rose and applauded wildly, and the doctor beamed. His sentimental verses pleased the guests as

much as they distressed Wendell. The new judge could hardly gather his thoughts to "say a few words" later.

The judgeship soon brought changes in the Holmes' daily living. With a salary of $6,000 a year, Fanny and Wendell need no longer live in rooms over a drugstore. Fanny found a house on Chestnut Street and furnished it in good taste. Wendell liked this home, and for the first time in his life he had the thrill of a modest success.

No longer must they dine in restaurants; they could have friends at home. Fanny arranged several small parties so the judge could enjoy good talk.

In the third year of his judgeship Holmes was invited to give the Memorial Day speech at Keene, New Hampshire.

Fanny went with him. Holmes thought the audience would be small, but he was glad to speak about the war, now twenty years away. Through these years he had come to believe that war, with its pain, hardships, and dangers — and its companionships — had been the greatest single factor in his education.

As he walked toward the stand on the village green, Holmes chanced to hear someone ask, "Why do we celebrate Memorial Day?" He began his speech with that question.

"Memorial Day celebrates and solemnly reaffirms from year to year a national act of enthusiasm and faith. To fight out a war you must believe something and want something with all your might. So must you do to carry anything else to an end worth reaching . . . You must be willing to commit yourself to a course, perhaps a long and hard one, without being able to see exactly where you will come out . . ."

He spoke of companions who had shared the hard course. Many had given their lives; others were living, doing useful work. As he talked, the May breeze stirred the flag over his head. People crowded close, wanting to hear every word in spite of that breeze.

". . . Through our great good fortune, in our youth our hearts were touched with fire. It was given to us to learn . . . that life is a profound and passionate thing . . . to scorn nothing but indifference . . . to see beyond the gold fields the snowy heights of honor . . . to learn that the only success which is man's to command is to bring to his work a mighty heart . . ."

The whole stirring speech was published in newspapers the next day and widely read. With it, Judge Holmes' reputation as a thinker and speaker was greatly increased.

In 1886 Yale University conferred an honorary degree of Doctor of Laws upon Judge Holmes. By an odd chance Oxford University conferred a similar honor upon Dr. Holmes that same day. He had taken Amelia along when he went to accept it. Father and son, the same day — an unusual honor for a family.

"Harvard should have given a degree to Holmes, ere this," someone at Yale remarked when the ceremony there ended.

"Eliot has not forgotten that Holmes left Harvard," was a quick answer. "Give him time — ten years maybe."

Those years of the 1880's brought many changes in Judge Holmes' personal life. Brother Edward died. Mother Holmes failed, and Dr. Holmes went about the house distracted without her. She died in '88; Amelia, widowed now, moved to the house to care for her father. Fanny went to see him daily and Wendell as often as he could.

Amelia lived but one year. Dr. Holmes was left alone in the tall house that he loved. As they walked home after the services, Wendell Holmes turned to his wife in despair.

"We cannot let him stay there alone, Fanny. What shall we *do?*"

"We shall do exactly as we have always tried to do, Wendell. We shall do what we think is right. Didn't you say you had to go to Pittsfield for a conference?" He nodded, miserably.

"When you return, come to the Beacon Street house. It will be all right, Wendell."

The next morning, after he had gone, Fanny walked

through their house that she loved. It had no nursery; no small fingermarks on the walls — she had accepted that. Now, without a tear or backward glance, Fanny put on hat and coat and went to 296 Beacon Street. She must see whether in that overflowing house there was any space at all for a few of their most treasured possessions. The rest must be got rid of somehow. Fanny was gentle and kind, but she was steel, too, when she had decided what was right.

In the next five years Judge Holmes' reputation for wisdom and for original thinking grew steadily, in the state and the nation. At home, he was still a young son.

"Where are you going, Wendell?"

"Whom did you see today?"

Dr. Holmes' keen curiosity, his eager mind, was active as long as he lived.

Judge and Mrs. Holmes stayed on in the old home. Their own was gone; they were used to this one. The judge was filled with energy and loved his work. If Fanny was lonely, she never mentioned it. She could always amuse herself.

The once "young" judge moved up as older men retired or died. The press began to quote his opinions — an unusual honor for a state judge. They called him a "liberal," that is, a judge who is willing to change from time-honored ways. Labor problems were news. Judge Holmes frankly said that since employers could get together, employees certainly could have a union; no worker should be discharged for being a member. He thought that peaceful picketing was within the law but that

violence in any form was intolerable.

Judge Holmes went to Europe on several short trips, usually alone. At first there was only money for one. "You must go, Wendell," Fanny said. "You need to see your friends; they inspire you." Later, she could not leave the doctor.

In the mid-nineties, Wendell and Fanny spent a summer at Beverly Farms, a place by the seashore beyond Salem. The nation was having a craze for bicycles; the judge got an American Hummer with a 70 gear — not the best for country roads, he discovered. It was not easy for a tall man past fifty to learn to ride — girls and boys in the neighborhood quite put the judge to shame. But he stuck at it.

A neighbor stopped his horse and buggy to watch Holmes climb out of a ditch and drag up his bicycle.

"Do you think it is right for a judge to ride a bike?" the man asked.

"Well," Holmes thoughtfully rubbed a bruised shin, "I'd say it depends on his build. Who'd you have in mind?"

Soon Holmes was riding five miles a day. The next week he rode twenty — and over *such* roads!

The nation continued to grow, by natural increase and by immigration. Chester Arthur was president, then Grover Cleveland and Benjamin Harrison — and Cleveland again — and McKinley. It seemed to Holmes as time passed people grew less interested in freedom and the Union, their country, and more interested in earning a living, for some a very good living. Industry, business, and labor grew too; Holmes thought that natural when the whole nation was growing so fast.

The judge read widely on all angles of public life, but he did not take "sides" because he thought it was the business of a judge to find justice for all — if he could do so. In twenty years he wrote some 1300 opinions; that is, he wrote out his reasons for decisions on that many cases. The majority of these were routine, but all needed deciding. His written opinions were short and to the point; he had a gift for getting at the heart of a case.

Soon after the brief Cuban war the chief justice of the court died, and the Governor appointed Wendell Holmes in his place. This new honor brought additional work. As chief, Judge Holmes must direct the work of the court; he must assign the cases to various judges for study and for writing out a summary of the court's decisions.

Then came the dramatic September of 1901. President McKinley was shot and the young vice-president, Theodore Roosevelt, was sworn in to the highest office in the land.

Change seemed to be in the very air.

The National Capitol

Judge Holmes Moves Up

15

Theodore Roosevelt had been president for less than a year when there was a vacancy in the United States Supreme Court. Mr. Justice Gray resigned because of his failing health, and it was the duty of the President to appoint another man to serve in his place.

This duty is also a privilege, one of the most important that comes to a president. He will want to appoint a man who will serve his country well and bring honor upon the president who chose him. He will want a man whose opinions about law and government are as nearly as possible like the president's own ideas.

The departing Justice Gray had had a long record of honorable service. He had been in the United States Supreme Court for twenty years. Before that, he had been a judge in the Supreme Court of Massachusetts, as Judge Holmes was at the moment. It was natural that the President should turn to Massachusetts for a successor.

No president has the time to follow carefully the work of the state courts. But Roosevelt knew that Holmes was spoken of as a "liberal," a man who was interested in justice in a changing world. Moreover, he had heard Holmes speak on several occasions and had read other speeches. Now he conferred with one or two friends about the beliefs and abilities of the Massachusetts judge.

As a result, the President sent Judge Holmes a letter of appointment to the United States Supreme Court. And on August 2, 1902, he announced his choice to the press.

Judge Holmes read the letter with strangely mixed feelings. Fanny nearly burst with pride at the honor to him.

"Oh, Wendell! You'll accept, won't you?"

"Well, I don't know, Fanny. We're happy here. I have the highest legal post in the state. You understand — the place in Washington is as associate justice, and very few associates are promoted to be chief justice — it seldom works out that way. I'm sixty-one. I'll have maybe ten years more of useful service. Would you like to spend those years in Washington? Or in Boston?" He looked at her thoughtfully.

A few years earlier, Fanny had had a long and serious illness, and she had not fully recovered. The doctors had insisted that she cut her hair and keep it short till she was stronger. She hated short hair. In a day when fashionable women could sit on their long tresses, she felt conspicuous. And the hair was gray. The very thought of Washington — that crowded, fashionable city, made her tremble. But Wendell should never know that.

"Washington, of course," she answered lightly. "It's the place for you! People are used to you here. There you will have a new and wider field . . ."

"But Fanny! You have not really answered my question. Will *you* like Washington?"

Fanny stared at him. Wendell was asking her to decide! She smiled — her old flashing smile that transformed her.

"You know, Wendell, there is one sure way to find out. Accept the appointment. Move there — then I'll know. And won't old Boston be surprised?"

So Judge Holmes wrote, accepting the place the President offered. This appointment must be confirmed by the Senate which was not to convene until December. But there seemed no doubt on that score.

Judge Holmes' change from the highest state court to the highest federal court brought out the dual nature of the judicial systems in the United States. The nation has two separate systems, one state, one federal.

Under its own constitution and laws, each state has a system of courts which have the power to decide almost any kind of case within the state. State courts are held in every city and town and county; they are the courts that citizens most often contact. State courts handle the bulk of ordinary legal business within the state.

The United States courts (also called federal courts) have power to decide such matters as are directly assigned to them under Article III of the Constitution. Cases where the federal government itself is a party, where two or more states conflict, or where citizens of two states are concerned, go to the federal courts.

In 1787 the makers of the United States Constitution set up the Supreme Court and gave to Congress the power to create more courts under it if any became needed. By 1900 there was so much judicial work that Congress had created many federal courts of appeal, and many district courts, all under the Supreme Court in Washington.

These early constitution-makers took the greatest care to make federal judges secure and free from personal and political pressures. They made three safeguards:

> A Supreme Court justice was appointed by the president (head of the executive branch) and confirmed by the Congress (legislative branch).
>
> A justice served until his voluntary retirement or death. He could be removed from the bench only by impeachment — a serious procedure.
>
> The salary of a justice could not be reduced during his service.

When Oliver Wendell Holmes' appointment to this high office and his acceptance became known, the newspapers commented favorably. A few editorials called him a "radical," which he was not. Holmes believed in steady growth and development, never in drastic change or sudden reform.

Fanny Holmes saved clippings. Some day they will know him better, she thought proudly.

Congress confirmed the appointment on the fourth of December. Expecting this, Holmes had rented a house facing Lafayette Square, a small park opposite the White House. He went at once to Washington as he was to begin work on the eighth.

"I wish you were going with me, Fanny," he said an hour before he left the house in Boston. " Why not get your hat and come along?"

"Because I didn't want packing cases and muss while you were here, Wendell — and now there is work to do — that's why," she said good-humoredly.

"Yes, I know." They had talked this over before. "After all, the taking of the oath is just a form — and you shouldn't make two trips in winter." He went on alone, only vaguely sensing the vast amount of work needed to empty that old house.

Irish James Doherty, Holmes' clerk and messenger in the Massachusetts court, went with him. They were to stay at the New Willard Hotel until the home on Lafayette Square was ready.

At the station gates, in Washington, they were met by an intelligent-looking, elderly colored man.

"I am John Graig," he said, introducing himself. "I was with Mr. Justice Gray. Now I am at your service, Mr. Justice Holmes."

Holmes was astonished — and thrilled as a boy. This was the first time he had been addressed by his new title. He turned and introduced Doherty and Graig.

"Graig is on to things here," Holmes added to Doherty. "He will tell me what to do. I'd like you to hunt up our house and be there when the coal we ordered is delivered. The house must be good and warm by the time Mrs. Holmes comes. With the big coal strike just settled, coal may be rarer than diamonds."

Graig went with Holmes to the hotel. Soon the new justice was off to make his call upon the President, and later, on a friend or two. He had just come back to the hotel when Doherty arrived, cold, weary, and mad.

"You can't get a thing done in this town," he blustered. "No Irish here. The coal company said they never heard of Oliver Wendell Holmes — who was he? It's a good thing, Judge, that Mrs. Holmes isn't here yet."

On the morning of Monday, December 8, Holmes, with John Graig as his guide, left the hotel for the Capitol.

At that time the United States Supreme Court convened in the room on the main floor of the Capitol that, until 1859, had been the Senate chamber. This room was the shape of a half circle, arched over by an ornate ceiling. The one straight side was marked by a row of marble pillars which gleamed white against rose-red draperies. In the center, above the pillars, was a golden eagle, its wings outspread. In front of the pillars were nine huge chairs and before these a long table, the judges' bench; to the left of this bench was the desk for the clerk; in front, sections for lawyers and their clients. Behind these were rows of seats for the public. It was a dignified and impressive room.

Holmes went directly to the robing room, across the hall. There the eight justices greeted him, and he put on his long black robe. There he took the oath to support the Constitution of the United States.

Then the clerk gave a signal, and the justices walked across the hall between silken ropes which held back crowds of people. The new justice walked last.

With his vivid sense of history, Holmes was deeply moved as he entered this room. Here Daniel Webster had stirred the nation with his eloquence. Here Henry Clay and John C. Calhoun had spoken. Holmes could all but hear the echoes of their words in the hush of this moment.

The eight justices took their places. Holmes waited with the clerk at the left end of the bench. As he turned slightly, he saw that the room was filled with people. He recognized the President's wife and daughter and other well-known people. He had not expected that the arrival of a new justice would have so much attention.

At a gesture from Chief Justice Fuller, Holmes stepped forward and laid his hand on the Bible the Justice held — the same book that had been used for John Marshall, Roger Taney and other justices in the 112 years of the court's history. A silence fell in the crowded room and Holmes began speaking the solemn words of the oath:

"I, Oliver Wendell Holmes, do solemnly swear that I will administer justice without respect to persons, and do equal right to the poor and to the rich, and that I will faithfully and impartially discharge and perform all the duties incumbent upon me as Associate Justice of the Supreme Court of the United States according to the best of my abilities and understanding, agreeably to the Constitution and laws of the United States. So help me God."

Silence hung for seconds after his voice stopped. Then the clerk motioned him to his seat at the left end of the bench. People stirred. The work of the court began.

Fanny arrived a few days later and found the house on Lafayette Square a mess of piled packing cases, but warm, wonderfully warm. "How did you do it, Wendell?" she asked.

"I didn't. Thank Doherty. He worked hard — do you know what one coal company said to him, Fanny? 'And who is this Oliver Wendell Holmes? Never heard of the man!'"

"Isn't that wonderful, Wendell!" Fanny turned to him, her eyes shining. "Now, and here, that name is all *yours!* You can make of it whatever you wish. I *knew* it was right for us to come here! I love the place already!"

Wendell Holmes followed her from room to room as she inspected the house and planned work to be done. Suddenly what he was saying caught her attention.

"You must come and visit the Court, Fanny! I wished for you on the eighth. You must come tomorrow!"

"*Tomorrow!*" Fanny caught her breath. Tomorrow. Hadn't the man noticed that there was something to do here?

Of course she went — and was thrilled with what she saw. He had known she would be.

The house was hardly settled when invitations to dinners began to arrive, the first from the White House. By a long tradition, the President and his wife always entertained for a new justice. Fanny dreaded the evening. What would she wear? How manage this awful hair? And what in the world did one talk about to a president?

"You look handsome enough for two, Wendell," she said
as they finished dressing when the evening came.

"You look well yourself," he teased. Luckily he did not
know that inside she was quaking, counting the hours till the
evening would be over. "Better open that box," he added.

On her dresser was a white box — surely not there a
moment before? She undid the string.

"Violets!" she exclaimed, burying her face in their fresh-
ness. "Where did you get violets — in December?"

"Oh, Washington is pretty wonderful," Holmes laughed.
"Pin them on, Fanny. The carriage is here."

As they walked into the drawing room at the White House
President Roosevelt came to greet them. Suddenly, Fanny

Holmes was not afraid. She took his arm, and he led her in to dinner. He loved to talk, and she was a perfect listener, giving wholehearted attention, speaking at just the right times.

The evening was a happy one. Fanny Holmes had the best time she'd had in years.

She was astonished to find that she was an immediate success in Washington. There were more invitations to dinner than there were days in each week. People called — and called again. Some distinguished visitor or other was always at her tea table where, word got around, there was sure to be good talk.

Fashion had never been one of Fanny Holmes' interests. She wore what she liked — and Bostonians had often been annoyed. In Washington, her independence was admired. The unusual was a mark of distinction.

"Who is that stunning woman?" strangers asked as she entered a drawing room. "Such carriage! Such grace!"

"That's Mrs. Holmes, wife of the new justice, you know."

Fanny bloomed under this approval. Her eyes glowed, and her health improved. She loved dining out, and people who sat near her found the slow changing of many courses oddly shortened. No one seemed to mind short gray hair. Fanny learned to tuck it under a net and forget it.

The move to Washington was a success for both the Justice and Mrs. Holmes. Now she must find a house they could buy and feel that they really belonged.

1720 I Street

Justice Holmes in Washington

The search for a home ended in the purchase of a high four-story brick, number 1720, in a row of houses on I Street. (Washingtonians often spell it Eye Street.) The capital city had many rows of such high narrow houses. Number 1720 was so like the Beacon Street house that its owners very quickly settled, and felt at home.

The large library, Justice Holmes' study, was the spacious front room of the second floor. Bookshelves lined the walls, and there the justice spent mornings and many evenings. In her sitting room behind the library, Fanny Holmes set up a case for her perfume bottles. She had several charming ones now, and her collection was growing. The justice revived his interest in art, and the rooms were brightened with charming water-colors which they found in little shops. Such changes did not happen all at once, but gradually, as the first rush of social life abated, and they had time for quiet pleasures.

One of the joys of Washington was the longer warm season,

the early spring, the lingering autumn. Fanny Holmes always loved birds and small creatures. Now she fed the early feathered visitors along with others who had dined at her window all winter. Rock Creek Park was beautiful the year around, and the Holmeses often drove there or visited the zoo.

Justice Holmes enjoyed the routine of his new work. After a leisurely breakfast, he went to his study, where he attended to mail and perhaps wrote an opinion on a case. Then he was off, walking the two miles to the Capitol.

Court convened from noon until four-thirty, with a break at two for a bit of luncheon. Holmes usually had a sandwich. Saturdays the court was closed to allow the justices to confer and make decisions. Sometimes work piled up so that court must adjourn for two weeks to allow the justices to do the studying needed to make wise decisions. Court closed for four months of summer.

Justice and Mrs. Holmes spent this season at Beverly Farms, but these months were not really vacation. Each justice must read hundreds of cases and decide which could properly be tried in the Supreme Court of the United States.

The government allowed each justice a modest sum for hiring a secretary to help with this year-around work. At first Justice Holmes wondered how to pick an aide. Then he passed the problem on to his old friend, John Gray, who was still teaching at Harvard Law School.

"Send me the pick of the current crop," Holmes wrote.

Gray chose carefully, a new man each year. The place was esteemed, for it was counted an honor to work for a justice and to have a year in Washington. Holmes' secretaries soon became a tradition.

Each autumn a bright young man arrived, bursting with pride and ambition. *He* had been picked from the whole class. *He* was going to help Justice Holmes do important work. The truth was quite a shock.

Mr. Justice Holmes looked up his own cases. He wrote his opinions in his clear Spencerian hand, learned in dame school. No typewriter was allowed in his study or in his hearing! The secretary was allowed to keep the Holmes' bank book in balance. Interest in the economics of John Stuart Mill did not include a liking for check stubs.

Each new secretary quickly learned to be on hand when the justice left for the Capitol. Holmes had a keen curiosity about everything and was a good talker as he walked. His remarkable memory ranged over a wide area. Now and then he dropped a sentence that the younger man never forgot:

"A *man* does not shift his misfortunes to his neighbor's shoulders; he overcomes them himself."

One day the question of choice of professions came up.

"Every calling can be great, son, when it is greatly pursued. But a man must choose; action controls the present. The thinker controls the future."

Mrs. Holmes mothered the young men as they came, one after another. She looked after their diets and their clothes. She invited their best girls and other friends to tea. She took them to parties at the White House and saw that they met interesting people.

"Drop in any time before 2 a.m.," she invited the young people. "After that hour you may find the lights out."

The constant stream of visitors to the Supreme Court amazed Justice Holmes. American citizens of all ages and from all walks of life came there. People from other lands visited the court, too, mingling with the Americans. They stood in the hall, as the nine justices crossed between the silken ropes. They filled the spectators' seats and listened for hours as cases were presented and argued.

"Unless I saw with my own eyes, I would never believe," Holmes remarked to Fanny one evening. "Today, people listened to a technical argument that would baffle a lawyer."

"They get comfort, knowing that someone there understands, that someone is guarding the nation and is trying to solve its problems. The justices are different from men in other branches of government; they are not trying to get elected. They are trying to find what is right."

Justice Holmes looked at her in surprise.

"You speak as though you had been there," he said.

"I was," Fanny admitted, blushing. "I go now and then. Every citizen should. I slip in at the back where I can watch the people as well as the Court. Reading the newspapers often makes me feel that the country is in a mess of graft, self-seeking.

"But in that highest court I feel that I am seeing statesmen. I know that often you do not all agree. But every one of those justices is trying. It makes me feel safe. And you do look handsome in a robe, Wendell. I wish your mother could see you."

The justices certainly did not always agree! Problems

brought to them covered a wide range of interests. A federal court was vastly different from a state court.

The relation of the federal government and business was becoming important. With every change of administration the federal government took on more power — was that good? The justices argued hours on such topics and did not agree. A final vote might be 6 to 3, or 5 to 4, with the majority deciding the case. The minority were called dissenters.

Soon after he joined the court, Justice Holmes dissented in a 5 to 4 vote on a railroad merger. The President was leading a popular crusade against trusts, and he considered the merger of two western railroads into the Northern Securities Company a trust. Justice Holmes thought of the merger as a "partnership . . . free from criminal intent to prevent competition." Trade unions, businesses, and even government were growing as the nation grew, he wrote. Size itself was not evil.

This opinion made headlines and was widely discussed. The President was annoyed with his new appointee, even though his own viewpoint won. Justice Holmes was not disturbed. He had taken an oath, a promise to the citizens, to do right as he saw it. Not even a president could influence him.

There were other dissents, for Justice Holmes' stand on social legislation was far in advance of his time. One, known as the Lochner case, made a stir. New York state had passed a bill to limit the hours a baker should work to 10 hours a day, 60 hours a week. The law was contested as a restraint of contract and came to the Supreme Court in 1905, where it was voted unconstitutional. Holmes dissented.

"A constitution (he wrote) is not intended to embody any particular economic theory. . . . It is made for people of differing views. . . . A reasonable man might consider this law a proper measure on the score of health, a first installment of a general regulation of hours of work." His opinion on this case gave encouragement to other social legislation.

Though he came to be known as the "Dissenting Justice," Holmes did not like to dissent; he thought over-use of the privilege might bring disrespect on the court. He voted with the majority in about ninety percent of the cases heard while he was a justice.

"Holmes uses his dissents for a double purpose," another justice remarked as a conference broke up. "He votes for what he thinks right on the case at hand. But he also hopes to alert the people. He wants citizens to ask, 'Is this a good law? Will it make for justice in our nation?'"

Those justices who worked together knew each other. They saw that Holmes was not for labor or capital, for property as against human rights, for a person or a state. As time went by many of his once startling dissents became accepted.

By way of resting him for such serious duties, Mrs. Holmes often planned interludes of fun. On a sunny afternoon one spring, Justice Holmes and his wife came down the steps of their home, dressed to attend an important formal party. The justice glanced at his watch.

"Fanny! We're much too early!" he exclaimed. Then he saw the mischief in her eyes. "You planned this! Well, what shall we do, lady?"

"Go to the zoo. You've neglected our friends there, Wendell. And the paper says there are new arrivals — among them a gorgeous tiger. Don't you want to see a tiger?"

Laughing, he handed her into the carriage.

They wandered around, seeing both new and familiar animal friends. They came to the tiger.

The lithe, handsome creature leaped at his bars and spat at the justice. Fanny laughed at his amazement.

Holmes, thinking to placate the tiger, stepped nearer. The beast growled and spat. His hair rose, his teeth gleamed.

Fanny eyed the scene, surprised. Animals always liked Wendell. Then she began to laugh again.

"Wendell, it's your tall black hat he hates. Take it off. Here, let me hold it."

Holmes lifted off the hat and handed it to Fanny. Instantly the tiger turned his disgust to her and roared viciously.

"Next time we come," Holmes said as he reluctantly turned away, "I shall wear my oldest clothes and *no* hat. That tiger has sense. He hates party clothes."

So with hard work, good friends, and many small joys, years passed.

During Justice Holmes' seventieth year, Chief Justice Fuller died. A new chief justice must be chosen for this administrative position. The matter was frankly discussed in the newspapers.

"Surely President Taft will appoint Justice Holmes," men said. "Not a man on the bench can compare with him."

"But no president should appoint a man who is about to retire. Remember, Holmes will be seventy next March."

That was evidently Taft's decision, too. For though he and Holmes were good friends, he gave the place to Justice White of Louisiana. Holmes understood. He did not like administrative work anyway. He'd discovered that while serving on the state court.

When his seventieth birthday came newsmen asked when he planned to retire.

"You can retire now, with full pay, Mr. Justice," one said, as though envious. The justice laughed; then he told them,

"I'll quit when work stops being fun."

When a close friend asked the same question, he answered thoughtfully, "I'll retire when God gives me the signal."

In 1910 Charles Evans Hughes was appointed an associate justice of the Supreme Court. Holmes found him congenial, and they enjoyed a close friendship. Six years later when Hughes resigned to be a candidate for president, Louis Brandeis, the young lawyer Holmes had known in Boston, was appointed in his place. Brandeis was an independent thinker, and with him Holmes had many stimulating talks.

War came, World War I that the slogans said was to end all wars. In its trail came suits involving other nations and peoples and many civil liberties cases. Justice Holmes was contemptuous of wire tapping — he called it "dirty business"; and in his dissent on the Abrams case he made clear his opinion on the right of free speech. He wrote:

"When men have realized that time has upset many fighting faiths, they may come to believe even more than they believe the very foundations of their own conduct that the ultimate good desired is better reached by free trade in ideas — that the best test of truth is the power of the thought to get itself accepted."

People were eager to hear the justice's opinions on new questions, and he had many invitations to speak. Holmes liked public speaking, but he felt it was unseemly for a justice to air his personal views. Invitations were declined.

The war ended. With 1921 came Justice Holmes' eightieth birthday. The air was clear and cool. Holmes and Brandeis walked home from the Court together, striding purposefully as they argued a case they were studying.

"What the world needs is not reformers, Louis," Holmes remarked. "It needs more civilized men."

Brandeis laughed and agreed.

At home Fanny was in the drawing room dressed in her best gray satin. Her hair, now white, was piled on the top of her head. Early violets pinned at her throat were fragrant and becoming. She sat in the big chair, graceful and erect.

"You won't like it, Wendell," she said quickly. "But if the cook is sick what can we do but go out for dinner? Get into your tails as quickly as you can — do, please!"

Holmes didn't like it. He stalked up the stairs, disappointed. He had been so sure that she would plan a party for him. Soon he was down, unappeased.

As he stepped into the room, the houseman folded back the doors into the dining room and there, around a beautifully set table stood twelve of his one-time secretaries, handsome in formal clothes, laughing at his astonishment.

"We thought you would *never* come!" one said in mock complaint, as the justice went around the table, shaking hands, slapping shoulders, welcoming his boys.

"Mrs. Fanny has been writing to us for months and now, when we got here, she hid us in the coal cellar till you should be ready!" He brushed coal dust from his broadcloth sleeve.

These men, each successful in his own field, had come from here and there over the nation to do him honor on his birthday. Holmes was so happy he could hardly eat!

The justice continued his daily walk to and from the Capitol until he was eighty-six. Then he rode in an automobile. His brief case was always packed with work. He seemed actually greedy for hard work, and his mental vigor was shown by his opinion in the Schwimmer case that year, 1927.

Popular thinking was stirred by his dissenting words in the court's 6 to 3 denial of citizenship to Rosika Schwimmer. Mrs. Schwimmer was a pacifist; she applied for citizenship and in taking the oath of allegiance to the country of her choice, she said she could not promise to bear arms in case of war. Holmes scathingly wrote that Mrs. Schwimmer was a woman, past fifty years old, who would not be allowed to bear arms if she wished to; and then he added:

"If there is any principle of the Constitution that more imperatively calls for attachment than any other it is the principle of free thought — not free thought for those who agree with us but freedom for the thought that we hate." Then the soldier of Civil War glories referred to the loyalty of other pacifists ... "Quakers have done their share to make the country what it is ... I had not supposed hitherto that we regretted our inability to expel them because they believe more than some of us do in the teachings of the Sermon on the Mount."

Fanny was not there to plan his ninetieth birthday celebration. She had died in 1929 and was buried in Arlington Cemetery. Holmes missed her terribly.

"She made my life poetry," he wrote to a friend.

So for March 8, 1931, friends arranged a radio party with a national hook-up, a novelty then. Justice Holmes sat by a microphone in his own study. He heard a program of praise of himself and his work such as few men ever hear. Charles Evans Hughes, back from the political field and chief justice of the Supreme Court; the president of the American Bar Association; and the dean of the law school at Yale — each gave a glowing tribute to the guest of honor.

After them, Wendell Holmes was to respond, the first time he had ever spoken into a microphone. What could one say after such speeches? Holmes' good taste made his words brief, a sincere "Thank you!" Listeners would remember the sentence, "Work is never done while the power to work remains."

On a wintry day months after that birthday evening, Holmes got "God's signal." Work had gone slowly; he had felt unlike himself, but had managed to finish the day's tasks, saying nothing of his new knowledge. He was driven home — and he never returned to the Court.

That same evening, January 11, 1932, he sent his resignation to the President.

With heavy responsibilities lifted from his shoulders, Wendell Holmes' strength seemed to be renewed. He read hours each day — newspapers, magazines, detective stories, Greek plays and Roman law in the original.

"Those Romans understood the importance of law," he remarked to the current young secretary. Law graduates still vied with each other for the chance to serve him. "They knew that civilization is held together by law. They knew that laws therefore are dangerous both when they lag behind social thinking and when they are too far ahead."

"Mr. Jefferson understood that, too," the secretary remarked. " 'When law is out of step,' Jefferson said, 'men lose
respect for it.' "

With reading, good talk, and letters exchanged between
friends, weeks and months passed quickly. Two days before
his ninety-fourth birthday, Justice Oliver Wendell Holmes died.
On the birthday, he was buried with a soldier's honors in the
National Cemetery at Arlington, Virginia.

When his will was read men saw that he divided half his
worldly goods among his nephew (Edward's son), his cousins,
several faithful servants, and two institutions — The Boston
Museum of Art and Harvard University. The other half, and
his home, he gave to the United States of America.

In the months after the death of Mr. Justice Holmes, American and English law journals issued special editions in his
honor. Words of praise included comments such as:

  · "The best judge America has produced."

"Good judges do not interpret the law; they make law by
their interpretations."

"He was a great Liberal but in no sense a radical; the stern
Puritan traditions of New England were in him, too."

Popular magazines also printed their praises:

"He gave people a new idea of law — not old rules, but a
growing, changing thing, helpful in each day's needs."

"Justice Holmes cared more for people than for property;
he understood the poor and he had the courage to stand against
the majority if he thought them wrong."

Justice Holmes was an associate justice, not chief, but

historians rank him as one of the great American justices. He had a vote in deciding about one third of all cases brought to the highest court from its beginning to the day he retired.

His life was dedicated to service. For three years he was a soldier; for twenty years a judge in his state; for thirty years a justice in the highest court of the country he loved. He brought to his work a keen intelligence, a shrewdness, a wide range of knowledge, a lively wit, a lofty vision — and a kind and honest heart.

With the passing of years, the fame of Mr. Justice Holmes has steadily grown. His genius with the written word has attracted countless readers of his letters and speeches and opinions, and has helped to place him high among the nation's heroes. He is honored as a wise philosopher, an honest judge, and a great man.

Supreme Court Building